Guided Reading
A How-to For All Grades

Bonnie Burns

Foreword by Jerry L. Johns

CORWIN PRESS
A SAGE Publications Company
Thousand Oaks, California

For information:

Corwin Press
A Sage Publications Company
2455 Teller Road
Thousand Oaks, California 91320
www.corwinpress.com

Sage Publications Ltd.
1 Oliver's Yard
55 City Road
London EC1Y 1SP
United Kingdom

Sage Publications India Pvt. Ltd.
B-42, Panchsheel Enclave
New Delhi 110 017 India

Printed in the United States of America

LCCN 2001089845
ISBN 1-57517-447-2

This book is printed on acid-free paper.

05 06 07 08 09 10 9 8 7 6 5 4 3 2 1

Dedication

To my mom, who taught me to persevere.

—B.B.

Contents

Chapter 1 — Guided Reading 1

Chapter 2 — Guided Reading and Read-Alouds in Kindergarten and First Grade 17

Chapter 3 — Guided Reading in the Primary Grades 31

Chapter 4

Guided Reading in Grades 3–12 79

Chapter 5

Looking at Questioning from Another Angle 97

Foreword

In *Guided Reading: A How-to for All Grades,* Bonnie Burns has written a practical volume that contains useful ideas for teachers at all grade levels. If you have lengthy experience in the field of reading, you will quickly see that guided reading is based on the Directed Reading Activity or the Directed Reading Thinking Activity. Individuals who have become teachers in more recent years or who teach content area subjects will find numerous strategies that can be readily incorporated into their ongoing instructional program.

Basically, the concept of guided reading means that teachers guide students through materials that are used for instruction. A critical foundation in guided reading is that students read materials at their instructional levels. During a typical lesson, students discuss both the content and the strategies they used to make sense of what is being read. Specific attention is devoted to levels of comprehension, questioning, before-reading strategies (e.g., picture walk-through, connecting the new with the known, setting purposes for reading), during-reading strategies (e.g., using cueing systems and fix-up strategies), and after-reading strategies (e.g., questioning, discussion, and summarizing).

The sample lessons for reading *Treasure Island* should be especially helpful for teachers in the upper grades who may be less familiar with the concept of guided reading. Lessons with content area texts may be very challenging because as Burns states, the texts "are often written above grade level." Burns does, however, provide several variations that can be used with content area texts.

Guided Reading is easy to read, and it has numerous blackline masters that can be used with students to help them understand the general process and the specific strategies that can be used in guided reading. Also included are tips for students who are not involved in the reading group and ways to use running records and miscue analysis to help energize instruction. Teachers who seek ways to support students as they move toward independence with texts will find help and support in *Guided Reading.* Many of the suggestions Burns offers can be incorporated into ongoing instructional programs. The result should be more highly engaged students who learn more strategies so they can understand and learn from texts.

Jerry L. Johns, Ph.D.
Emeritus, Northern Illinois University
President-Elect, International Reading Association

Introduction

Guided reading has recently been a hot topic in the literacy instruction field. Some question if it will pass as just another pedagogical fad that produces few results. That is unlikely since good reading teachers have been using guided reading techniques for years. Since Socrates, teachers have used questioning to help their students explore texts in greater depth. Maybe teachers just called guided reading by a different name, such as "stopping to question" during reading. Maybe they used techniques from Russell Stauffer's (1969) Directed Reading Thinking Activity (DRTA) or hints from the teacher's manual. Teachers in the past did not always make students as consciously aware of their reading strategies as teachers do now—a significant change.

There is no computer program, workbook page, or blackline master that can duplicate the benefits of teachers reading with their students to help them clear up misconceptions, connect ideas, and decide which strategies are most useful for the task at hand. Guided reading is a technique in which teachers guide students through reading by selecting a text; providing students with a purpose for reading the text; supplying background knowledge to prepare students to read the text; having students silently read the text; stopping to discuss the text during reading to clear up any misunderstandings; and asking students content as well as strategy questions to ensure students' comprehension.

Guided reading is a technique in which teachers guide students through reading by:

- selecting a text;

- providing students with a purpose for reading the text;

- supplying background knowledge to prepare students to read the text;

- having students silently read the text;

- stopping to discuss the text after reading to clear up any misunderstandings; and

- asking students content and strategy questions to ensure students' comprehension.

There is no computer program, no workbook page, no blackline master that can duplicate the benefits of teachers reading with their students to help them clear up misconceptions, connect ideas, and decide which strategies are most useful for the task at hand.

Teachers must become skillful guides and learn how to ask the right questions. Several methods and techniques for guided reading have been developed by researchers and specialists to help teachers. *Guided Reading: A How-to for All Grades* presents the best basic methods of guided reading, applies them to different grade levels, and provides several variations of these methods so teachers can adjust instruction to the changing needs of readers.

Guided reading in the primary grades has been widely discussed in current literature and is reviewed here as well. The methods of guided reading for intermediate, middle, and upper grades, however, have received little attention even though the students in those levels need to learn comprehension strategies the most. Several chapters in *Guided Reading* are devoted to methods for intermediate, middle, and upper grades, though most are not widely known or used in classrooms. Advanced comprehension techniques, an emphasis on critical thinking as the final step of comprehension, and an entire chapter on guided reading in the content areas and with expository text—especially difficult for many students—are all gathered in this book.

Try these techniques with your class and be sure to try them more than once. It takes practice to become skillful in questioning, to identify difficulties in the text, and to focus on content and reading strategies simultaneously. Guided reading bridges direct instruction and independent reading. May this book be the bridge from the frustration of not knowing how to help readers who do not comprehend to the confidence of competently developed lessons that help students learn solid content and reading strategies. May your students all become expert readers.

How to Use This Book

This book is intended for K–12 classroom teachers. Although teachers' interest in certain chapters will depend on what grades they teach, every teacher should read chapter 1, which develops the basic premise for guided reading with general guidelines. Any teacher who reads aloud to their classes will enjoy chapter 2. Chapter 3 is geared to primary teachers and chapter 4 is targeted to teachers in the intermediate, middle, or upper grades. Chapters 5 through 7 give invaluable information to teachers of any grade level. The following highlights each chapter's features.

Chapter 1, Guided Reading, first defines guided reading with a clear explanation of what it is and how it works compared to other classroom reading patterns. Teachers who have used mostly oral reading or silent reading and follow reading with questions will find that guided reading offers an alternative that lends itself to teaching comprehension strategies while using the texts that students are reading. The chapter also includes suggestions about when to use guided reading and which students will benefit the most.

Chapter 2, Guided Reading in Kindergarten and First Grade: Read-Alouds, introduces the kindergarten and early first-grade version of guided reading: the interactive read-aloud. The many benefits of reading aloud can be enhanced with strategy instruction throughout the interactive read-aloud. Teachers will also find that the students are more engaged when given the opportunity to respond actively during read-alouds.

Chapter 3, Guided Reading in the Primary Grades, shows how important leveled books and smaller groups are at this stage. Sources for finding good books and finding lists of already leveled books are provided. Reading cueing systems are explained, and skills and strategies for first-grade reading are enumerated. Literacy activities for students not in the guided reading group are suggested as well as ideas for how to organize the literacy time block. Instructions for running records—used to document achievement and diagnose strengths and weaknesses of young readers—are given in detail.

> **Teachers who have used mostly oral reading or silent reading and follow reading with questions will find that guided reading offers an alternative.**

Chapter 4, Guided Reading in Grades 3–12, takes the reader through the guided reading process step by step and incorporates a sample guided reading lesson for the middle grades. Questioning strategies for targeting specific reading skills are outlined. (I spent most of my years teaching students at these grade levels. I could always tell the power of guided reading because when we came to end-of-book reviews, it was always the sections with which we did guided reading that the students had the best recall and understanding.)

Chapter 5, Looking at Questioning from Another Angle, compares traditional levels of questioning and levels of comprehension with a different yet parallel system of questioning. This alternate system provides clues to learners about which strategies should be used to find answers. This chapter also includes a primary example of using questioning at all levels during a guided reading lesson.

Chapter 6, Variations on Guided Reading, explains how teachers can modify the guided reading process with techniques such as Directed Reading Thinking Activity (DRTA), prediction with the overhead, using visualization as an aid to comprehension and recall, think-alouds, and reciprocal reading. It also explains techniques of the virtual guided reading teacher—strategies that can be used to guide readers when the teacher is working with other groups.

Chapter 7, Guided Reading with Content Textbooks, explains why students have such difficulties with textbooks even though they seem to read fiction with ease. The chapter gives several suggestions for using guided reading with content textbooks and includes modified guided reading techniques such as ReQuest, Questioning the Author (QtA), and Talking Drawings. Teachers of all grades will relate to the difficulties that students encounter with textbooks.

Blackline masters included at the end of each chapter may be used to facilitate guided reading. Some may be posted in classrooms to help students anticipate the steps in guided reading or to better understand the levels of questioning. They may also serve as a reminder to students of what they need to do when reading independently to be active, engaged readers. The Daily Agenda icons in chapter 3 help young children understand the agenda of literacy activities. Suggestions for classroom use are included for all blackline masters. Feel free to adopt or adapt as needed.

Students need reading instruction at all grade levels. They require the help and guidance of an expert reader, the teacher. As text becomes more difficult at the upper grades and comprehension becomes all-important, students need more instruction, not more assignments. Guided reading is one of the ways to provide that instruction while using the texts that students are reading. Guided reading makes thinking visible and students find immediate application for the strategies they are learning. Teachers across all grade levels can benefit by adding guided reading to their repertoire.

Guided Reading

Instruction enlarges the natural powers of the mind.

—HORACE

In the past, there have been two major organizational patterns for reading in the classroom: oral reading and silent reading. Many of us remember round-robin oral reading. The teacher assigned paragraphs to be read orally, usually calling on students in order down the rows. However, there are problems with students reading only one paragraph each. Instead of listening to the others, students sometimes practiced their upcoming paragraph, daydreamed while others read, or passively read along. By the end, students gained very little comprehension of the whole passage, and frequently experienced very little practice in reading. Perhaps the class discussed the content, but dialogue about the strategies that students used or could have used to comprehend was often brief.

In silent reading, all students were assigned to read the entire passage themselves. This was better than round-robin reading, when students may have only paid attention to one paragraph because at least silent reading exposed students to the entire passage. After reading, students were usually expected to answer questions. Unfortunately, if students did not understand the selection, the question period was too late to discuss problems or strategies. Students who did not understand the passage could not answer the questions, which led them to feeling discouraged and frustrated. When reading skills were taught, teachers traditionally used separate texts as sample exercises for each skill, hoping students would be able to transfer the skills to real text later on.

The Benefits of Guided Reading

Guided reading is the bridge between direct reading skills instruction and independent reading. It is the stage where teachers guide and support students while they are constructing meaning. During guided reading, students read silently as their teachers read right along with them. Teachers provide guidance and prompting as students try out reading strategies and discuss the process of comprehending written text. Guided reading is the vehicle through which readers practice and learn comprehension strategies within the context of literature or other authentic text.

Guided reading occurs while students are reading and invites discussion of both content and reading strategies (see Figure 1.1 for an overview). With guided reading, the teacher first selects a relatively short passage for students to read. The passage length depends on students' grade level and abilities. It may be just one paragraph or a few pages. In guided reading, students read material at their instructional levels. While independent-level materials can be read successfully without any teacher intervention or guidance, instructional-level materials require new or unpracticed reading strategies that present obstacles to students reading on their own. Second, the teacher sets a purpose for reading the passage. Third, the teacher discusses new concepts, background, or reading strategies that the students will need to know. Fourth, students are given enough time to read the passage silently.

Fifth, after the students read the passage, the teacher discusses content and reading strategies with the class. It is very important that the discussion covers both the content and the strategies students used to comprehend the passage. If they are not both included, the discussion becomes just a question-and-answer session about the content or diverts to a direct reading skills instruction lesson. Finally, the teacher asks comprehension questions. Students prove their answers by finding the relevant passage in the text. Teachers can ask students how they reached certain conclusions. If students make predictions, they should relate the information they used to form those predictions. The class might evaluate the content or apply it to a new situation. During guided reading, the teacher might ask a variety of questions to help students monitor their general comprehension using several strategies or he or she might ask students to focus on a single reading strategy that is critical to the selected passage. This active participation in the reading process increases both interest and success.

> **Guided reading is the bridge between direct reading skills instruction and independent reading.**

The Guided Reading Process

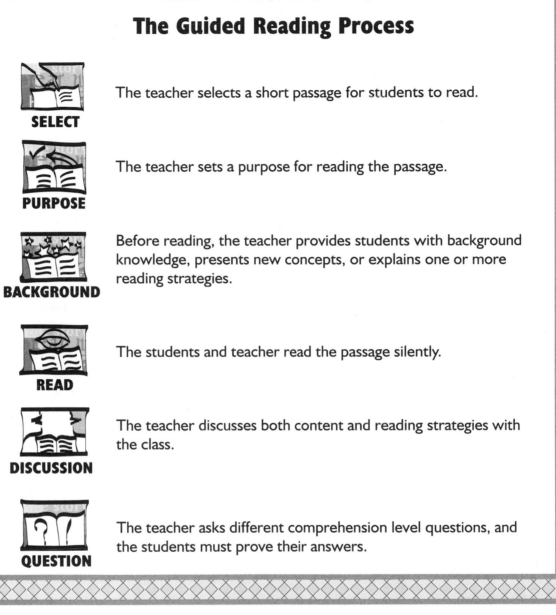

SELECT — The teacher selects a short passage for students to read.

PURPOSE — The teacher sets a purpose for reading the passage.

BACKGROUND — Before reading, the teacher provides students with background knowledge, presents new concepts, or explains one or more reading strategies.

READ — The students and teacher read the passage silently.

DISCUSSION — The teacher discusses both content and reading strategies with the class.

QUESTION — The teacher asks different comprehension level questions, and the students must prove their answers.

Figure 1.1

After students have read the first passage and discussed it, the process starts again. The teacher sets another purpose and provides background knowledge. The students read another section silently, the class discusses additional content strategies, and the teacher asks new questions. This whole process helps make thinking visible. Students solve problems during reading, rather than at the end (or not at all!). It is a time for practicing old and new strategies with an expert, the teacher, guiding the process. The class proceeds in this manner until it has read the entire selection or until the teacher feels confident that the students can proceed independently. The procedure moves along rather slowly, but it is a process rich with opportunities for students who are learning comprehension strategies.

Of course, guided reading is just one part of a balanced reading program. Other parts of the reading program include whole-class instruction, small-group instruction, direct instruction, and independent reading. Word study, either word attack or vocabulary, and first-time use of a new reading strategy usually take place as separate activities prior to guided reading.

Guided reading can be implemented with both fiction and nonfiction texts and is relevant for any grade level.

Guided reading can be used for monitored practice and support in all of the following aspects of comprehension:

◆ reading for a purpose

◆ predicting and confirming or rejecting

◆ finding information

◆ connecting prior knowledge

◆ monitoring and adjusting strategies

◆ visualizing

◆ summarizing

◆ organizing information according to text structure

   – topic/subtopic

   – cause and effect

   – comparison and contrast

   – sequence, problem/solution

◆ making inferences and connections

◆ thinking about implications

Scaffolding

Guided reading can also be called a Scaffolded Reading Experience or SRE (Graves and Graves 1994). Providing scaffolding means giving support that enables students to accomplish tasks that would otherwise be beyond their efforts. Difficult tasks require more scaffolding or guidance, and less difficult tasks require a small amount of guidance. If the task does not require any guidance, it can be assigned for independent reading.

One strength of SRE and guided reading is flexibility; they allow the teacher to select reading strategies according to either the needs of the students or the special requirements of the text. For example, students might need background knowledge to understand a new concept. Seventh graders who are studying the continental drift theory may benefit from pre-reading and during-reading discussions of text about layers of the earth's crust. Other teaching strategies can be chosen based on the characteristics of the text.

When reading a short story that includes a flashback, students may profit from a discussion of how a writer handles shifts in time, such as with an extra line space in the text or time clues like "It was in the summer of 1962 . . ."

One of the important roles of the teacher in guided reading or SRE is deciding where and when to provide support. Determining a level of support is a diagnostic and analytical process based on reader needs and text characteristics. Timely discussions of critical background information or authors' techniques provide a scaffold or support mechanism that helps students comprehend a text they might not have understood if they had read independently.

The SRE framework is broader than the guided reading framework because it includes more extensive support in both the pre-reading and post-reading stages. Teachers can use the Checklist for Choosing Guided Reading Strategies (see Figure 1.2) to decide which skills the reader needs to learn or to assess which features of the text may require scaffolding.

> **Guided reading provides a scaffold or support mechanism that helps students comprehend a text they might not have understood if they had read independently.**

High Engagement

Guided reading is extremely helpful to students who seem to read without thinking or just read to get to the end of the text. These students have an opportunity to experience making comprehension the primary activity during reading, and they have a teacher to guide the process. Guided reading is also rewarding for students who have difficulty focusing on printed material for a sustained period of time. During guided reading, students are prompted to recall, think about, or apply what they have read at regular intervals; no student can read passively for very long. Readers receive expert leadership and direction from the teacher as to what they should pay attention to while reading silently. They are given a defined shorter period of time for concentrated reading. Guided reading is also particularly useful for very difficult passages, such as those that contain new concepts, difficult sentence structure, or require inferences.

Checklist for Choosing Guided Reading Strategies

Comprehension Strategies Students Need

❑ Connecting prior background

❑ Recognizing concepts

❑ Visualizing

❑ Monitoring comprehension

❑ Predicting

❑ Forming questions

❑ Using organizational patterns
  • cause and effect
  • sequence
  • comparison and contrast
  • topic/subtopic
  • problem/solution

❑ Summarizing or retelling

❑ Identifying main ideas

❑ Using fix-up strategies

❑ Inferring

❑ Generalizing or drawing conclusions

❑ Evaluating

❑ Enjoying

Obstacles Presented by Text

❑ Complicated sentence patterns

❑ Unfamiliar concepts and settings

❑ Unstated emotions

❑ Unusual time patterns (e.g., flashbacks)

❑ Unexpected change of narrators

❑ Organizational patterns
  • cause and effect
  • sequence
  • comparison and contrast
  • topic/subtopic
  • problem/solution

❑ Graphic aids
  • maps
  • graphs
  • charts

❑ Text aids
  • preview sections
  • summary sections

❑ Interrupted plot or disjointed information

Figure 1.2

Although some researchers (Fountas and Pinnell 1996) define guided reading as being conducted only with small groups, the process is suitable for whole-class instruction, especially beyond the primary grades. Even when used with an entire class, guided reading encourages high student engagement, because everyone reads with a purpose and is ready with an answer or an opinion. Older students can write some or all of the answers to ensure high involvement and on task behavior. As students read the next section silently, the teacher can check on the written responses of various students.

Another way the teacher can ensure high engagement during guided reading is to call on all students equally, regardless of ability or achievement. Having equal opportunities to respond was found to contribute to higher student achievement in the Teacher Expectations and Student Achievement (TESA) study sponsored by the Phi Delta Kappa organization. The study found that "students with poorer learning histories are often called on less, giving them less opportunity for involvement" (Joyce and Showers 1995, 80). Gradually, these students became less involved and felt less valued. Calling on every student every day improves the climate of the class and keeps students on their toes. Students know they will be expected to respond at some time during the class, and they know their answers will be valued.

> **During guided reading, students are prompted to recall, think about, or apply what they have read at regular intervals; no student can read passively for very long.**

TEACHER QUOTE

" Guided reading gives students a focus or purpose for reading. As they read, they are guided to think about how and why something happens in the story. Thus they are learning the 'habit of mind' of metacognition—thinking about their own thinking. Students are encouraged to think critically and make connections to their own lives. It also helps students develop skills for life and should also make them better test takers. Maybe one day we will be able to throw away the test practice books and use good literature and guided reading to help students prepare for the tests! "

—Robin Finnan-Jones
Academic Intervention Specialist-Reading Teacher
PS 16 Corona, Queens, New York

Chapter One Summary

Guided reading promotes thoughtful reading. It provides students with an opportunity to learn and practice comprehension strategies as they read real text. It broadens students' ideas of what it means to read and gives them an opportunity to participate in monitored practice at all levels of comprehension. As students read and discuss, they receive support and clues from an expert reader to guide them through the process. Guided reading also breaks down the text into manageable lengths so students can concentrate on limited content and strategies. Best of all, guided reading gives students practice with a variety of questions so they can learn to ask their own questions during independent reading.

TEACHER QUOTE

❝ It is impossible for me to believe that children can achieve an effective level of reading comprehension without expert guidance. Early readers in my classes always responded well to guided reading lessons when the questions were challenging and within their experience. When young children in my Early Childhood classes were asked to gather facts, formulate opinions, or predict outcomes of a story, they exhibited a greater interest in further exploring literature. Their independent writing soon reflected the communication skills and strategies successfully developed from these guided reading sessions. ❞

—Penny Denton
Educational Consultant
Flushing, NY

Chapter 1 Blackline Masters

◆ Guided Reading Process Icons

- Select
- Purpose
- Background
- Read
- Discussion
- Question

◆ Ideas for Classroom Use

- Make overhead transparencies of the icons. Before using guided reading with your class, discuss the process, and show each icon as you describe each step.
- Post the Guided Reading Process Icons on the reading bulletin board for students to become familiar with the steps.
- Paste each photocopied icon onto a piece of posterboard; hold up the appropriate icon to remind students what they should be doing at that time.
- Make overhead transparencies of each icon. During guided reading, show the appropriate icon to remind students what step they are working on.

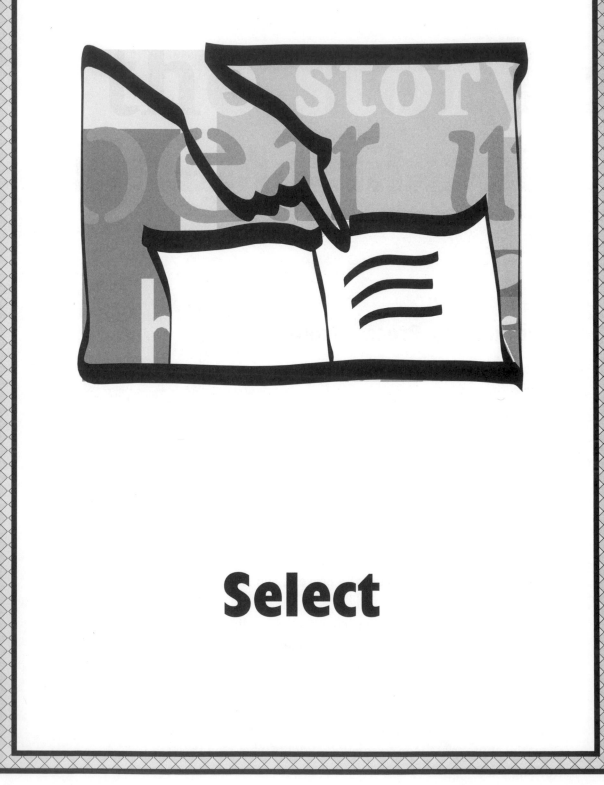

Select

Purpose

Background

Read

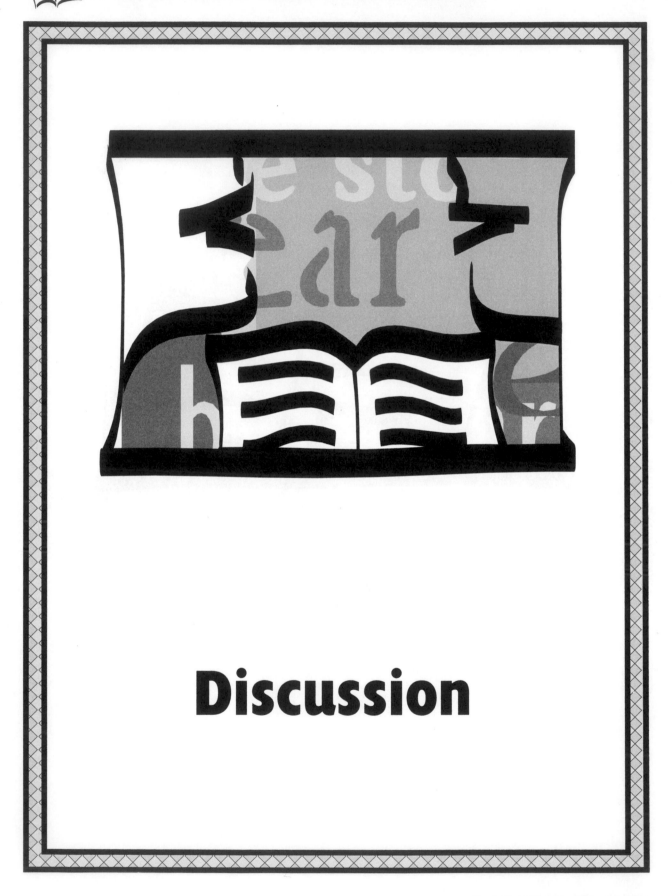

Discussion

Question

Guided Reading and Read-Alouds in Kindergarten and First Grade

CHAPTER 2

Soft as some song divine, thy story flows.
—HOMER, THE *ODYSSEY*

Reading aloud has always been an important activity for kindergarten teachers and for first-grade teachers at the start of the school year. Students begin to understand the process of reading and discover that the marks on the page stand for written speech. They begin to learn left-to-right progression, up from down, and that spaces are put between words rather than between syllables. They hear the more formal structure of language that is found in books rather than the informal structure of conversation. Students learn a sense of story—beginning, middle, and end—and they also learn a wealth of new information and vocabulary. When the teacher reads the story in a fluent and expressive manner, the students learn how an accomplished reader sounds. When teachers read aloud, kindergartners and first-graders learn the joys of literature in addition to learning many other emergent literacy skills.

Interactive Read-Alouds

When teachers read stories straight through and dialogue only at the end of the reading, they promote passive listening and limit the opportunities for discussion of early reading strategies. Read-alouds can be structured to invite greater student participation and engagement. They can also be used to guide students through the first steps of becoming strategic readers. Guided reading can begin as early as preschool or kindergarten using interactive read-alouds (Barrentine 1996). Nearly all of the thinking processes involved in making meaning during reading can be replicated during listening coupled with active involvement. During the read-aloud, students interact with the text, with the teacher, and with peers as the teacher asks questions throughout the story to encourage discussion of content and construction of meaning. The interactive read-aloud allows an opportunity to discuss both content and reading strategies as the story progresses.

An interactive read-aloud proceeds in much the same manner that any guided reading lesson does (see Figure 2.1). First, the teacher chooses a story. Then the teacher introduces the story and asks students to describe what they see on the cover or first page and predict what the story might be about. The teacher can ask the students to begin making connections to what they already know, such as a similar setting or another book by the same author. This background step gets students into the topic or story line of the book, demonstrates how to make connections to their own lives, and shows how illustrations can be used to further understanding. All of this proceeds in a casual, relaxed manner that is compatible with storytelling.

When teachers read aloud to students, kindergartners and first-graders learn the joys of literature in addition to learning many other emergent literacy skills.

As the teacher reads the book, he or she stops periodically to ask for reactions to the story from the students. They discuss the story line, but the teacher also consciously guides students to use strategies for constructing meaning that they will eventually use when reading by themselves. All levels of comprehension and questioning—literal,

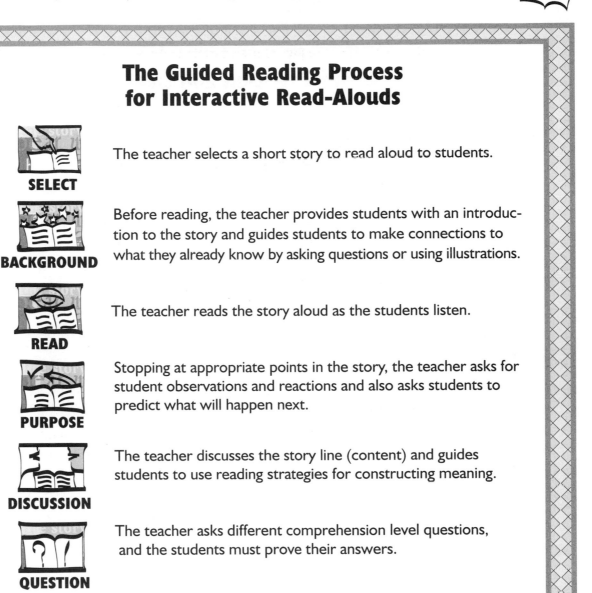

The Guided Reading Process for Interactive Read-Alouds

SELECT
The teacher selects a short story to read aloud to students.

BACKGROUND
Before reading, the teacher provides students with an introduction to the story and guides students to make connections to what they already know by asking questions or using illustrations.

READ
The teacher reads the story aloud as the students listen.

PURPOSE
Stopping at appropriate points in the story, the teacher asks for student observations and reactions and also asks students to predict what will happen next.

DISCUSSION
The teacher discusses the story line (content) and guides students to use reading strategies for constructing meaning.

QUESTION
The teacher asks different comprehension level questions, and the students must prove their answers.

Figure 2.1

literal rearranged, inferential, and critical—can be used with young students. *Literal* questions have answers that can be found right in the text. *Literal rearranged* questions have answers that are also found in the text but do not appear all in one place, such as a sequence of events. *Inferential* questions require the readers or listeners to combine their own experiences with the text to draw a conclusion or make an inference. *Critical* questions require answers that are beyond the text and call for an evaluation or application. (Levels of questioning and comprehension are discussed in greater detail in chapter 5; also see Figure 2.2.)

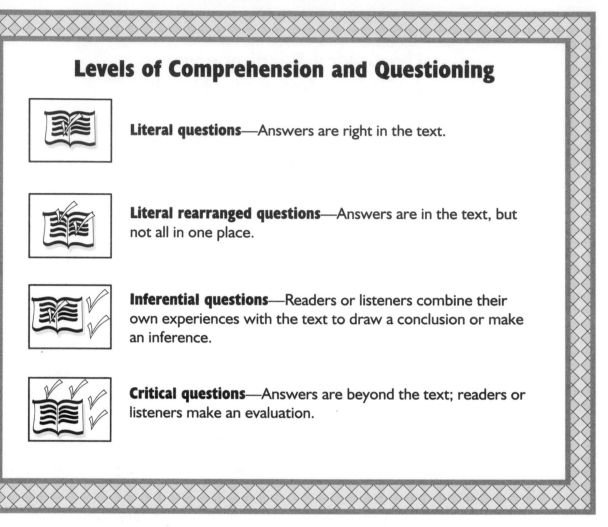

Levels of Comprehension and Questioning

Literal questions—Answers are right in the text.

Literal rearranged questions—Answers are in the text, but not all in one place.

Inferential questions—Readers or listeners combine their own experiences with the text to draw a conclusion or make an inference.

Critical questions—Answers are beyond the text; readers or listeners make an evaluation.

Figure 2.2

At the literal level, the teacher can ask content questions about story structure and plot, character reactions and changes, print features, and vocabulary. To lead students to the reading strategy they used, the ever-present question is "How did you know that?". Students might respond by pointing out a feature in the picture or repeating a line from the story.

At the literal rearranged level, the teacher can encourage cause-and-effect thinking. The teacher might ask questions such as "Now why would Mr. Blodgett say that?" and then ask students to cite the parts of the story where they found the cause.

Listeners involved in the read-aloud love to predict. The teacher can ask students inferential questions such as "What do you think will happen next, and why do you think so?". The class can discuss if the prediction is likely to be true based on what has already happened. Students can interpret characters' feelings by saying a line the way a character might when exemplifying surprise, fright, or delight. The teacher can help students interpret language by asking what a character meant by saying "I'm all thumbs."

Critical questions can help students learn to apply story knowledge to their own lives. The teacher can ask if the students have been in similar situations or what they might have done if they had encountered the same situation.

When teachers make mistakes, purposely or not, they can think aloud about what did not make sense and how they can correct their thinking so it does make sense. When asked to help their teacher restore meaning, students use strategies for making language meaningful and are exposed to early fix-up strategies. Young students delight in absurdities and are often glad to help teachers see silly mistakes!

All in all, the teacher points out aspects that might otherwise be overlooked. Young students have so much to learn that their attention often flutters from point to point—the pictures in the book, the words on the page, the content of the story, a classmate's foot, the teacher's bracelet. Interactive read-alouds keep students engaged in the content of the story. Students' attention is refocused in short time segments with the opportunity to respond to each section of the story. They are also involved in the process of reading, which helps maintain their focus. Students have an increased realm of what to think about as they listen to the teacher's questions and observe the answers and reactions of their classmates. They have an opportunity to become personally involved in the story and to work at solving the problems of meaning rather than simply listening passively.

To guide students to use reading strategies, teachers can ask certain questions. Teachers should be sure to use all levels of comprehension and questioning. Following are some examples:

◆ What does Mr. Blodgett do? (literal)

◆ Now why would Mr. Blodgett say that? (literal rearranged)

◆ What do you think will happen next, and why do you think so? (inferential)

◆ What would you do if you were Mr. Blodgett? (critical)

To lead students to discover the reading strategy they used, the ever-present question teachers should ask is:

◆ How did you know that?

Mixing Instruction and Storytelling

Teachers must maintain a balance when encouraging interactions and still keeping the plot of the story in mind. Personal anecdotes that wander too far from the story can interrupt the text as can too many clues about strategies. Most teachers are quite comfortable mixing storytelling, discussion, and hints and cues about comprehension strategies, but some teachers are uncertain of exactly what mix to use. How much interaction should occur and which strategies should be emphasized? How can all the parts be naturally interwoven? Pinpointing a few focus strategies can help teachers keep the conversation on track so they maintain the balance between story appreciation and conversation about process. See Figure 2.3 for steps on planning an interactive read-aloud.

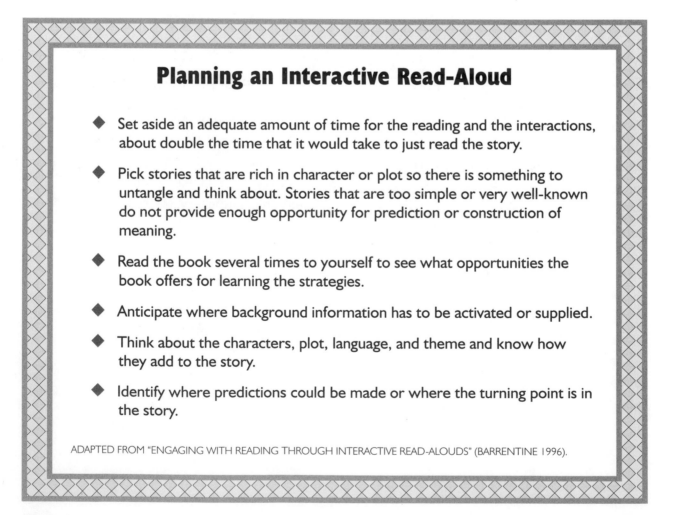

Planning an Interactive Read-Aloud

◆ Set aside an adequate amount of time for the reading and the interactions, about double the time that it would take to just read the story.

◆ Pick stories that are rich in character or plot so there is something to untangle and think about. Stories that are too simple or very well-known do not provide enough opportunity for prediction or construction of meaning.

◆ Read the book several times to yourself to see what opportunities the book offers for learning the strategies.

◆ Anticipate where background information has to be activated or supplied.

◆ Think about the characters, plot, language, and theme and know how they add to the story.

◆ Identify where predictions could be made or where the turning point is in the story.

ADAPTED FROM "ENGAGING WITH READING THROUGH INTERACTIVE READ-ALOUDS" (BARRENTINE 1996).

Figure 2.3

Teachers should be prepared to deviate from their plans (Barrentine 1996). A student's observation or question might be more relevant or offer an opportunity for learning that had not been previously considered. Some stories elicit many personal observations. Teachers should be prepared to allow students to share multiple personal stories after the reading. It is those connections that make the book relevant.

The authors of the National Research Council report, *Preventing Reading Difficulties in Young Children,* also encourage interactive read-alouds. They found interactive read-alouds especially important for students who had little storybook experience outside of school (Snow, Burns, and Griffin 1998). They recommend adding nonfiction books to the storybook list of read-alouds and modifying the types of questions used to match the different genres of read-alouds. A 1989 study by Mason and colleagues asked kindergarten teachers to read storybooks, informational texts, and easy-to-read picture books. Depending on the genre, the teachers' behaviors automatically changed. Before reading a storybook, the teachers discussed the author, main characters, and concepts. During reading, they clarified vocabulary and engaged the students in making predictions and explaining motives and events. After reading, they asked the students to reflect on the meaning and message of the story. With science texts, the teachers used different interactions to help their students relate the text to their everyday lives. They asked students to predict and explain and to determine and test causes. Vocabulary work emphasized concept development rather than simple synonym definition. With the easy-to-read picture books, discussion was more limited but focused on the print and words on each page. These books seemed more promising for teaching word recognition, as they were less complex and there was less need for solving problems in comprehension.

> **Young students have so much to learn that their attention often flutters from point to point. Interactive read-alouds keep students engaged in the content of the story.**

Chapter Two Summary

The interactive read-aloud helps kindergarten and first-grade students become acclimated to the many processes that occur simultaneously in reading. The teacher alerts and guides students so they learn that reading is an active process that draws both from the text and from the reader. Students are kept on track with compelling books, background discussion, structured read-aloud sessions, and different levels of questions that spark interesting discussion and introduce content and reading strategies to young readers.

TEACHER QUOTE

" I'm glad I get to teach in the 21st century—so much has changed since I began in 1970.

In the 70s when I began teaching, I was told that I was cheating when reading aloud to my third grade students. They should read on their own. Little did we know the power modeling had to motivate children to read.

Teaching began as a struggle to break away from the controlled vocabulary of the basals, to expand writing in the elementary grades, and to capitalize on the potential for learning with open-ended questions, student-chosen reading materials, student-generated research topics, writing and reading aloud.

When I began teaching, silent sustained reading was wasting time. My colleagues said kids can read on their own time at home. Now I see students begin reading in the classroom, and taking the books home to read more. "

—Pat Braun, Reading Specialist
6th Grade Teacher
Roosevelt School, River Forest, IL

Chapter 2 Blackline Masters

◆ Levels of Comprehension and Questioning Icons

- Literal
- Literal Rearranged
- Inferential
- Critical

◆ Ideas for Classroom Use

- Before your first guided reading session, explain the four types of questions displayed in the blacklines. Use overhead transparencies or icons pasted onto posterboards to emphasize each type of question as you explain them.
- Post icons on the reading bulletin board for students to consult to as you use guided reading.
- Photocopy icons and paste to posterboard; hold up the appropriate icon during questioning as a prompt to students. (You can cover the definitions.)
- To adapt these strategies for older students, you might distribute copies of the icons and ask students to write sample questions for each level.

Literal Questions

Answers are right in the text.

Literal Rearranged Questions

Answers are in the text, but not all in one place.

Inferential Questions

Readers or listeners combine their own experiences with the text to draw a conclusion or make an inference.

Critical Questions

Answers are beyond the text; readers or listeners make an evaluation.

Guided Reading in the Primary Grades

My early and invincible love of reading,
I would not exchange for the treasures of India.

—EDWARD GIBBON

Guided reading in the primary grades allows the teacher to provide guidance and support while young students are reading. In the primary grades, the teacher works with small groups of students who are reading at approximately the same level, use many of the same strategies, and have many of the same needs (Fountas and Pinnell 1996). The book or text should be at the students' instructional level: easy enough to read, but difficult enough to provide some challenges in word identification, comprehension, or content.

A Typical Guided Reading Session

SELECT

First, the teacher selects a book. The book should be short enough so that students can read it in about five to ten minutes. (If the text is longer, such as an early chapter book, the teacher can split it into parts and continue cycling through the remaining steps on following days, reading and discussing, and reading and discussing.)

PURPOSE

After selecting the book, the teacher introduces it to the group. Each student should have a copy to read. The teacher does a picture walk-through, previewing some of the language and pointing out several features in the pictures or certain words that are critical to the content. The students become familiar with aspects of the story; the information is already on the tips of their tongues when they encounter the print. This naming of objects and reviewing of essential language is especially important for students learning English as a second language. The teacher asks students to comment on things they notice so that their background knowledge is brought to the foreground and they can begin making connections between what they already know and what they are about to read. If some concept is new or unfamiliar to several students, the teacher might provide additional background. The pre-reading discussion in guided reading removes many potential obstacles.

BACKGROUND

READ

Each student then silently—or at least quietly—reads the whole book. As the students read silently, the teacher observes, carefully noting which strategies each student is using. Some students may easily understand the story, and the teacher will notice them confidently proceed through the pages. Students who encounter a difficult word may go back to the beginning of a line or finish a line and return to an unknown word to see if context will help. The teacher might hear a student use phonetic clues to try to decode a new word. Students using picture clues will look back and forth from the text to the pictures. Students having difficulty may appear frustrated with trying to discern the meaning of the text on the page, and the teacher is available to help on the spot. The teacher should note these behaviors and use them to diagnose strategies that the students are using.

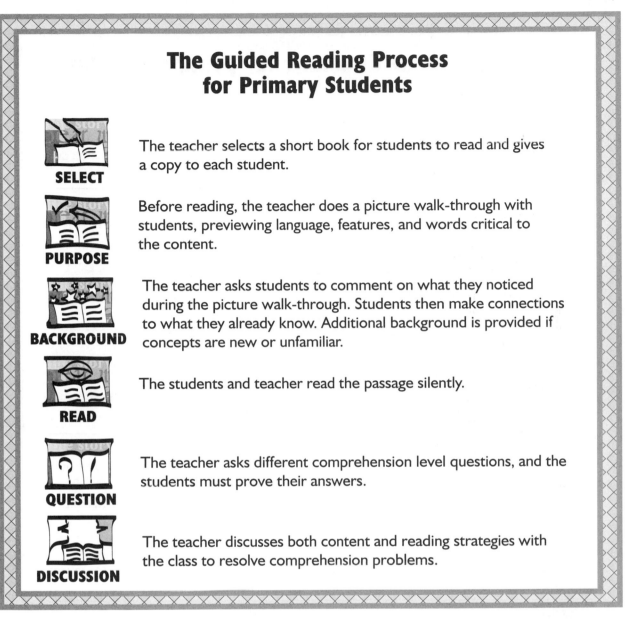

The Guided Reading Process for Primary Students

SELECT — The teacher selects a short book for students to read and gives a copy to each student.

PURPOSE — Before reading, the teacher does a picture walk-through with students, previewing language, features, and words critical to the content.

BACKGROUND — The teacher asks students to comment on what they noticed during the picture walk-through. Students then make connections to what they already know. Additional background is provided if concepts are new or unfamiliar.

READ — The students and teacher read the passage silently.

QUESTION — The teacher asks different comprehension level questions, and the students must prove their answers.

DISCUSSION — The teacher discusses both content and reading strategies with the class to resolve comprehension problems.

Figure 3.1

After the students have finished reading, the teacher asks questions. The teacher can ask students to give their reactions to the story or to retell the beginning and the end, or a single event. Students can relate what they liked or disliked about the story. Students' answers may reveal that what seemed like an easy read did not result in total comprehension. Misunderstandings can be cleared up, and those misunderstandings can be used to diagnose the students' reading strategies and future needs. (See Figure 3.1 for an outline of the process; see Figure 3.2 for a sample checklist of behaviors to look for in primary students developed by Patsy Clark of Niagara Falls, New York. A blackline master is also provided at the end of this chapter.)

QUESTION

Sample Behavior Checklist for Primary Students

(Circle the appropriate number.)

Focus

Involved in assignment				Off task
5	(4)	3	2	1

Head and Body Movement

Limited movement				Much movement
5	4	3	(2)	1

Feet still				Tapping
5	4	(3)	2	1

Comfortable				Slouching, wiggling
5	4	3	(2)	1

Facial Expression

Involved, interested				Frustrated, bored
(5)	4	3	2	1

Shows emotion appropriate to content				Emotionless
(5)	4	3	2	1

Eyes

Left-to-right sweep				All over page
5	(4)	3	2	1

Checks picture/text				Skips picture/skips text
5	(4)	3	2	1

Lips

Reads silently		Mouths words		Letter by letter sounds
5	4	(3)	2	1

Hands

Holds book at appropriate distance			Distance indicates vision problem	
5	4	(3)	2	1

Finger points in sweeps across page		Finger points word by word		Frames word with fingers
(5)	4	3	2	1

Speed of Completion

Fast				Slow
5	4	(3)	2	1

ADAPTED FROM PRIMARY OBSERVATION CHECKLIST DEVELOPED BY PATSY CLARK.

Figure 3.2

This is also the time for teaching word recognition strategies in context or for teaching problem-solving strategies. If the teacher noticed that a certain word or text feature in the story gave several readers trouble, students can be asked to return to that particular page. The teacher may choose to emphasize a particular word that can be used to build other words in a word family. The teacher may also purposely look for examples of short vowel words or irregular sight words. The teacher might want the students to connect the story to their own lives, notice how the resolution to the problem was accomplished, or decide if the story was fantasy or reality. Teachers should seize the teachable moment and guide the students through those words, sentence patterns, or content that caused difficulties. Other response or extension activities may also be used, but they are not necessary for every text.

DISCUSSION

Once the students have been guided through the book and are successful with it, their teacher can add the book to the collection in the independent reading corner so the students may read it again and again, alone or with a buddy. Occasionally, guided reading groups reread a story to offer additional practice and give the students confidence and increase fluency. Rereading familiar materials and then moving on to more difficult pieces is a technique consistently used in Reading Recovery.

After the teacher sends the group off to reread the book with partners or to do another activity, the teacher usually asks one student to stay behind to take a running record. A running record is an individual diagnostic assessment. The student reads a new passage aloud and the teacher makes a written record of the student's reading, noting errors. This individual observation gives the teacher an insight into the student's strategies and provides information for which strategies should be taught next, emphasized now, or re-taught. It also helps determine the student's reading level so the teacher can evaluate group placement. Each time the group meets, a different student reads for the teacher. Soon each student has had an opportunity and the running records accumulate, providing continuous documentation of each students' progress. The method for taking a running record is discussed later in this chapter.

Teachers should seize the teachable moment and guide the students through those words, sentence patterns, or content that caused difficulties.

Finding Good Books

Finding interesting primary trade books can be a pleasant task. Several Web sites can help teachers review children's literature. All of the following Web sites review literature and give recommendations, and several offer suggestions for teaching with literature.

The Children's Literature Web Guide
www.acs.ucalgary.ca/~dkbrown

Children's Book Links
http://absolute-sway.com/pfp/html/childrens.htm

The Children's Book Council Online
www.cbcbooks.org/

Children's and Adolescent Literature Resources
www.indiana.edu/~eric_rec/comatt/childlit.html

Carol Hurst's Children's Literature Site
www.carolhurst.com

Finding a sufficient number of books that can be successfully read by emergent readers has always been challenging. Trade books (commercially published books) and little books have met that need. Little books are usually eight to sixteen pages long, and many are available through the Wright Group, Rigby, Sundance, and Dominie Press. Several publishers of basal readers are also using sets of easy books as part of their basal program. However, when ordering books, teachers need to have specific goals in mind; some easy books emphasize decodable text, some emphasize high-frequency words, and others are pattern books.

Choosing Books at the Right Level

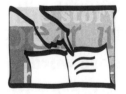

SELECT

During guided reading, teachers help students access increasingly difficult texts. Beginning readers come to school with a wide variety of language and reading experiences. Some are lucky enough to have been read to and have substantial experience with print. They are already comfortable with stories and the language used in books. Other students have had little exposure to reading. Teachers should create groups consisting of students at the same level of reading (see Figure 3.3).

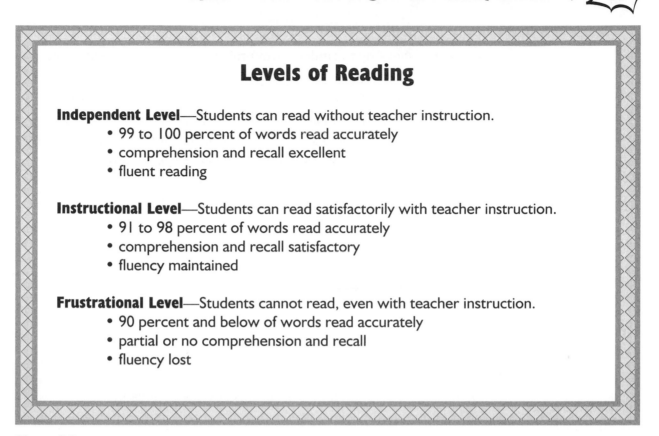

Levels of Reading

Independent Level—Students can read without teacher instruction.
- 99 to 100 percent of words read accurately
- comprehension and recall excellent
- fluent reading

Instructional Level—Students can read satisfactorily with teacher instruction.
- 91 to 98 percent of words read accurately
- comprehension and recall satisfactory
- fluency maintained

Frustrational Level—Students cannot read, even with teacher instruction.
- 90 percent and below of words read accurately
- partial or no comprehension and recall
- fluency lost

Figure 3.3

It is very important to choose books at the instructional level of the students if students are to be successful. They should be able to read over 91 percent of the words accurately, which is considered instructional level (see Figure 3.3). The instructional level is the stage where students can do satisfactory reading provided they receive pre-reading or during-reading supervision and instruction from the teacher. Comprehension and recall are at a satisfactory level. When students can read 99 to 100 percent of words accurately, they are considered to be at the independent level. At this level, students can read easily and fluently without assistance. Both comprehension and recall are good. When students can only read 90 percent or fewer of the words, they fall into the frustrational level. Students lose fluency at this level. Comprehension and recall are partial, and students show signs of discomfort. If students cannot read over a 90 percent accuracy level, it is too difficult for them to obtain the meaning of the story. They struggle with so many unknown words that the story becomes disjointed, they lose the connections between print and sense, and they miss out on the joy of reading.

There are important benefits to text that is at the appropriate level. When the text is just about right, students can problem solve as they read. They have enough clear and sensible information to figure out the few missing pieces. It is almost like puting together a jigsaw puzzle. Five hundred loose pieces lying on the table invite almost random placement of the pieces. But when the picture starts to become clear, the assembler can begin using problem-solving strategies such as looking for certain items, colors, or outlines. The process is much the same with beginning readers.

> **When the text is just about right, students can problem solve as they read.**

Selecting books at just the right level can be a daunting task. Many delightful children's books that are perfect for read-alouds are not perfect for beginning readers.

The work of identifying books by level has been done by other authors. Consult the following books for help in identifying appropriate leveled books:

◆ *Guided Reading: Making It Work,* by Mary Browning Schulman and Carleen deCruz Payne (Scholastic 2000), lists 650 titles leveled by reading age and Reading Recovery standards.

◆ *Best Books for Building Literacy for Elementary School Children,* by Thomas G. Gunning (Allyn and Bacon 2000), annotates each book and divides books into easy, average, and difficult reads for grades 1–6.

◆ Irene Fountas and Gay Su Pinnell have a leveled list in *Guided Reading: Good First Teaching for All Children* (Heinemann 1996) that includes both trade books and little books for students in grades K–4. The beginning levels of books each fall within a narrow range of reading difficulty while books on the upper end have a wider range.

◆ For those teachers without access to multiple copies of little books or trade books, Parker Fawson and D. Ray Reutzel have published a list of stories in five basal readers for kindergarten through grade 2. The readings are leveled according to Reading Recovery guidelines. The list can be found in the September 2000 issue of *The Reading Teacher* (International Reading Association).

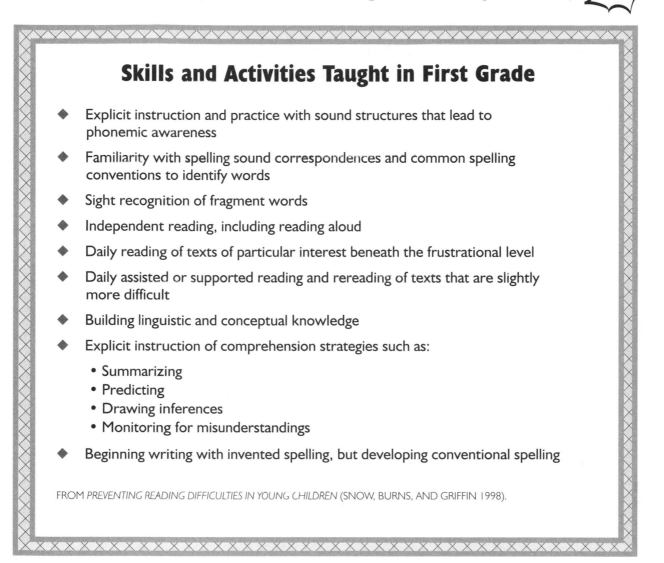

Skills and Activities Taught in First Grade

◆ Explicit instruction and practice with sound structures that lead to phonemic awareness

◆ Familiarity with spelling sound correspondences and common spelling conventions to identify words

◆ Sight recognition of fragment words

◆ Independent reading, including reading aloud

◆ Daily reading of texts of particular interest beneath the frustrational level

◆ Daily assisted or supported reading and rereading of texts that are slightly more difficult

◆ Building linguistic and conceptual knowledge

◆ Explicit instruction of comprehension strategies such as:

  • Summarizing
  • Predicting
  • Drawing inferences
  • Monitoring for misunderstandings

◆ Beginning writing with invented spelling, but developing conventional spelling

FROM *PREVENTING READING DIFFICULTIES IN YOUNG CHILDREN* (SNOW, BURNS, AND GRIFFIN 1998).

Figure 3.4

Primary Skills and Strategies

Once the books have been found, what do teachers need to teach in primary reading? Let's start with a review of the big picture in reading. A primary teacher's first goal is to help beginning readers understand that reading is a process of constructing meaning. The students need to know that there is a grander purpose to reading than just figuring out what sound the letter *w* makes. The National Research Council report, *Preventing Reading Difficulties in Young Children* (Snow, Burns, and Griffin 1998), provides a recommendation for the design of first-grade instruction (Figure 3.4). Many of these skills can be accomplished during guided reading, especially during daily reading of texts at the instructional and independent levels.

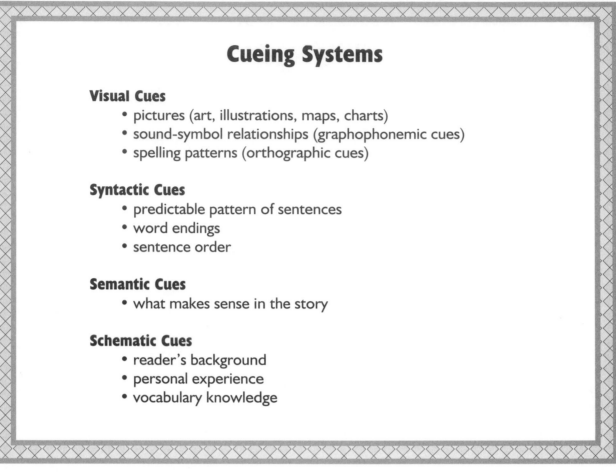

Cueing Systems

Visual Cues
- pictures (art, illustrations, maps, charts)
- sound-symbol relationships (graphophonemic cues)
- spelling patterns (orthographic cues)

Syntactic Cues
- predictable pattern of sentences
- word endings
- sentence order

Semantic Cues
- what makes sense in the story

Schematic Cues
- reader's background
- personal experience
- vocabulary knowledge

Figure 3.5

Cueing Systems

To accomplish teaching these skills to students, it is critical for the teacher to understand how readers process text and create meaning. A widely accepted framework is cueing systems, which includes visual cues, syntactic cues, semantic cues, and schematic cues (see Figure 3.5).

Visual Cues

New readers rely heavily on visual cues. Beginning books tell a significant part of the story through pictures, reducing the amount of text to be mastered. Older students and adults also use pictures in textbooks, magazines, and newspapers, especially when the content is unfamiliar. The pictures often add an emotional element that words can hardly express. Readers also use sound-symbol relationships (graphophonemic cues) and spelling patterns (orthographic cues) to identify new words. Beginning readers encounter more never-before-seen words to identify than adults do, but adults still use graphophonemic and orthographic cues to pronounce new names and unfamiliar words. Graphophonemic and orthographic analysis, plus a lot of practice, help readers transform unfamiliar words into sight words.

Syntactic Cues

Syntactic cues concern the predictable pattern of sentences. Most sentences contain predictable patterns of nouns, adjectives, verbs, and adverbs, as well as prepositional phrases. Although the following sentence is composed mainly of nonsense words, many questions can still be answered by using the predictable pattern of the sentence.

> ### The squitley tourmarands vashornly blained the cloughts in the wroked knanflede.

What kinds of tourmarands were they? What did the tourmarands do? How did they blain the cloughts? Where did this take place?

Word endings also give the reader cues, as does the order of the sentence. With the sentence Bobby put the toy on the _____, the beginning reader knows that the unidentified word has to be a noun even if the designation noun is not known. If the reader sees Bobby put the toy on the t_____, the two cueing systems used—looking for a noun that starts with the letter t— may lead the student to guess that the word is *table.* When he sees the *b* and the *l,* the reader can verify his or her guess.

Semantic Cues

Semantic cues are the clues about what makes sense in the story. Most readers know that what they are reading should be logical. Bobby would probably put the toy on the *table* and not on the *tuna* or the *teaspoon.*

Schematic Cues

Schematic is derived from the word *schema,* meaning background. Schematic cues include all of the reader's personal background and vocabulary knowledge. The beginning reader probably does not know the words *thesaurus* or *telespectroscope* and would not guess them. If the text did name *thesaurus* or *telespectroscope* as the unlikely resting place of the toy, the young reader would not understand where the toy was because those concepts are not within his or her experience. Teachers continually activate or build schema when they teach new concepts and new vocabulary.

> **When students read silently and discuss the story during guided reading, they learn that comprehension and sense are fundamental.**

Readers need to use and integrate all the cueing systems to comprehend. Comprehension requires all of the cueing systems and a few more skills besides. All readers use these skills, but beginning readers rely more on some of the cueing systems than expert readers do. Readers also need to be fluent (or quick) so they do not forget the beginning of the sentence before they get to the end. Most of all, readers need sufficient practice to thoroughly learn these skills and integrate them into the reading of whole text. Guided reading does not exclude any of the cueing systems or skills, although it clearly concentrates on building comprehension through the daily reading of texts at the instructional and independent levels. It certainly also includes building linguistic and conceptual knowledge and explicit instruction of comprehension strategies.

Skills Taught Outside of Guided Reading

Although all reading skills and strategies can be practiced and prompted during guided reading, not all are taught exclusively within guided reading. Teachers will teach some skills and strategies directly while indirectly teaching or practicing other skills through guided reading. Guided reading is just one part of a balanced primary reading program. Other parts of the reading program include whole-class instruction, small-group direct instruction, teacher read-alouds, shared reading, independent reading, word study, opportunities to write independently and with others, and opportunities to work in activity centers.

Other skills can be specifically taught and practiced outside of guided reading, such as the "working with words" part of the day. There is not a commandment that says "Thou shall teach nothing in isolation." It is often necessary to teach how words fit into sentence patterns to explain sound-letter correspondences and word family patterns, and to work on sight words in isolation so that readers get the basic idea of how the strategies work. A National Research Council report states that outstanding teachers present "explicit instruction for reading and writing, both in the context of 'authentic' and 'isolated practice' " (Snow, Burns, and Griffin 1998, 196). This kind of word study can often be done in whole-class lessons or through writing. One interesting study combined guided reading with Project Read, a multisensory approach to teaching word recognition with at-risk primary readers (Bruce, Snodgrass, and Salzman 1999). The approach was not only compatible, but successful.

Word recognition is essential to comprehension but does not guarantee understanding. However, there is very little understanding if the reader cannot recognize the words. Keith Stanovich (1993/94) puts the relationship into perspective:

> Children who begin school with little phonological awareness have trouble acquiring alphabetic coding skills [phonics] and thus have difficulty recognizing words. Reading for meaning is greatly hindered when children are having too much trouble with word recognition. When word recognition processes demand too much cognitive capacity, fewer cognitive resources are left to allocate to higher-level processes of text integration and comprehension. (281)

Stanovich continues with what he calls the Matthew effect, derived from the gospel according to Matthew, which is commonly paraphrased as the rich get richer and the poor get poorer. Students who have trouble with comprehension find reading unrewarding, which leads to less involvement in reading activities. They get less practice, read at slower rates, and learn less vocabulary and content than do students who read voluntarily and widely. Of course the opposite is true, up to a point. Those who learn phonemic awareness learn sound-symbol relationships more easily so they can identify new words quickly. Word recognition requires less concentration, so more effort can be put into comprehension. Comprehension strategies must still be taught, however, because good word recognition, while essential, does not guarantee comprehension.

Guided reading is the time when all the skills come together and are applied while reading. When teachers are right there with students during reading, they can provide immediate support and reminders about strategies that the student might not remember or know. When students read silently and discuss the story during guided reading, they learn that comprehension and sense are fundamental.

Developing Problem-Solving Strategies During Guided Reading

When a cueing system does not work for a student, the teacher can intervene and ask:

◆ What in the picture would help?

◆ What would make sense?

◆ What would fit into the sentence?

◆ What would match the sound of the beginning letter of the word?

◆ What is most likely to happen next?

To help students to access different problem-solving strategies, teachers may say:

◆ Look at the picture. Does what you read match what they are doing?

◆ Does that sentence sound right?

◆ Does that look right?

◆ Does that word end with the same letters as another word you know?

◆ Read that sentence again and see if that fits in with the story.

◆ Read that word again and use the sound of the first letter of the word.

◆ What else could you do to make that make sense?

Reading continuous text, that is, an ongoing story, is often easier than learning individual words because the reader can use multiple cueing systems. When students read continuous text during guided reading, teachers can help them try different problem-solving strategies when the cueing system that readers depend on most does not work. When a reader gets stuck, the teacher can step in and ask questions or make statements that leads the student to other strategies.

A variety of questions from the teacher help students access different strategies so they do not come to rely upon just one strategy. With small groups, it is possible to ask the right question at the right time. Other students in the group can also learn to give clues rather than just tell the answer.

Fix-up strategies are perfect for guided reading discussions when something does not make sense. Meaning can become disjointed when students misread a word or interrupt a phrase. Frequently, students notice a mismatch between known language patterns and what they have just read, but they are not sure how to correct the mismatch. When teachers notice this mismatch, they can prompt students to use several strategies, teaching them questions they can ask themselves as readers. The teacher prompts students to use multiple strategies and apply fix-up strategies to a problem—both characteristics of good readers.

Discussions After Reading

The discussion after reading not only helps the teacher gauge if the students understood the story, but also helps students develop higher-level reader response strategies. In addition to answering literal questions about the story, the discussion should also lead students to respond to the text in open-ended and personal ways. "Most of the time with the group is spent in discussion, in appreciating and enjoying the language of literature, and in sharing personal and group insights" (Routman 1991).

The teacher can show readers how to apply strategies that good readers use. Connecting the text to prior knowledge and experiences students have in their own lives is one method. It is always easier to learn something new when connected to something already known. Students do not always make this connection independently, so the teacher might ask, "Does your little brother do that, too?" or "Have you ever seen a snake up close?" The information in the text becomes more accessible and more sensible when it is linked with prior experiences. Prior knowledge also helps in making predictions and judging whether what was read makes sense. When the teacher helps students attach information during a guided reading discussion, the connection can be made on the spot, and students learn to use the strategy themselves during independent reading.

To prompt students to use fix-up strategies, teachers can say:

◆ Did that make sense?

◆ Read that again.

◆ Tell me what is happening now.

◆ Read to the end of the sentence and see if it makes sense.

◆ Is that what you thought would happen?

◆ You are close, but try it again so it sounds right.

◆ What do you know about this topic?

◆ What does not seem right?

The short discussions at the end of a story in a guided reading group also provide students with reinforcement of attitudes. The social interaction in a discussion about reading is very rewarding as students share their opinions about a book. Reading is such a solitary and internal activity. Even as adults, we love to have a good chat about a book we are reading and share our joys or insights. The pleasure of exchanging views in a small group about a book we have enjoyed is difficult to duplicate in whole-class activities. In small groups, students listen to one another, share their successes in reading a book, and learn that perseverance pays off.

Organizing Guided Reading Groups

Dividing the class into four groups works well for organization. The groups that contain readers who are just beginning to read can be smaller than groups of students who are well on their way. Students are initially grouped by the level of text that they can successfully read. Grouping remains flexible so students can move according to individual progress. Typically, two guided reading groups meet each day for fifteen to thirty minutes, each of the four groups meeting with the teacher a total of two to three times a week. The youngest readers read an entire book during this time; more advanced students may require several sessions to complete a longer book. It is recommended to schedule five minutes between groups so the teacher can circulate within the classroom to solve any problems that have arisen and to keep groups working efficiently (Borgert 1998).

> **It is essential that students are engaged in other meaningful activities involving literacy and not just busywork.**

When meeting with groups, the youngest and most flexible teachers often sit on the reading rug surrounded by supplies, including a write-on chart or a pocket chart. Teachers with less flexible bodies use a small table with students sitting to the sides and across from them. Every experienced primary teacher I know can read upside down as well as right side up. Teachers should be sure to position themselves so they have an unobstructed view of the other students who are pursuing independent activities.

Activities for Students Not in the Guided Reading Group

When the teacher is occupied with a guided reading group they often wonder how students working independently can make the best use of their time. It is essential that students are engaged in other meaningful activities involving literacy, not just busywork. Teachers usually have small groups of four to six students rotate among a variety of literacy activities. The grouping for these activities need not be the same as the guided reading groups. The independent groups may be homogeneous or heterogeneous.

Two key concepts for a smoothly functioning classroom include a self-directed system for following the agenda of activities and explicit teacher direction for how to function at each activity. Teachers frequently use a Daily Agenda Board with durable picture icons to denote the activities for the day (see Figure 3.6 for a sample Daily Agenda Board and Figure 3.7 for a list of independent activities). The icons can be clothespinned to charts, attached by Velcro strips, or placed in a large pocket chart. Whatever the form of the chart, it should be easy to rearrange the activity cards for each day's schedule. The names of the students in each group can be posted at the top of the list of icons. The students work at the tasks in the order that they are posted on the agenda. When different groups are at different tasks, there are enough materials for everyone and a variety of literacy skills can be practiced each day. Quieter and noisier activities can be balanced. Students usually do three or four independent tasks while the teacher works with the guided reading groups. As individual students finish, they can move to the next center. It is not necessary for the entire group to move together.

> **When teachers are right there with students during reading, they can provide immediate support and reminders about strategies that the student might not remember or know.**

The second key to a smoothly functioning classroom is for students to function independently at each activity. They need to know how long they are expected to stay or what task they must complete. The teacher needs to establish a system for handing in work other than personally delivering it to the teacher. Students need to learn to ask other students when they are puzzled or figure out an alternative by themselves. At the beginning of the year, the teacher should introduce one or two stations. The more modeling, demonstration, and practice the teacher offers, the more comfortable the students will be working independently. For example, the teacher may need to show students what partner reading means and how students can read with their partners in several different ways. Tasks as simple as showing the picture on a page to a reading buddy may need to be spelled out. While productive classrooms are often noisy, students must learn to be considerate of others who are in the reading group or who are trying to concentrate on an independent reading passage.

Sample Daily Agenda Board

Group 1	Group 2	Group 3	Group 4
Bobby	Jose	Linda	Isaac
Jimmy	Lauren	Tommy	Julie
Mike	Rogelio	Irma	Dolores
Latisha	Thurmond	Kathleen	Katie
Marilyn	David	Yen	Lee
Betty	Irene	Alberto	Frank
Shenise	Kevin	Jason	Jenny

Guided Reading

Guided Reading

Guided Reading

Figure 3.6

Independent Activities for Daily Agenda Board

 **Independent Reading**—This is always included as one of the activities. Students read books that groups have read, leveled books in browsing baskets, illustrated content books, or other informational books.

 **Partner Reading**—Each student reads to the other, each student reads every other page, or both students read together in chorus.

 **Listening Center**—Students use headphones to read along with a book on tape.

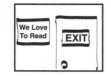 **Reading Around the Room**—Students quietly walk around the room and read labels, word walls, charts, etc. (Primary classrooms are filled with labels, word walls, and charts.)

 **Writing Center**—Students can label pictures, retell the story, or write in their journals.

 **Word Study Activities**—Partners or groups can use flash cards, play concentration games, or Go Fish games, use letter cards to make words, or practice rhyming words.

 **Poetry Center**—Students can read poetry, patterned books, or nursery rhymes.

 **Art Center**—Students can draw pictures of what they read, make collages, or illustrate their writing journal entries.

Figure 3.7

Independent Activities

 Independent reading is always one of the activities. Teachers can store the books that groups have read in baskets, using a different color basket for each group. Baskets should include multiple copies of titles the students have read. In addition, teachers can place other books in the basket that they are confident the students will be able to read. By providing leveled browsing baskets, teachers can ensure success during independent reading. In addition to the baskets intended for each group, illustrated content books and other informational books may be placed in a general basket. Because of its technical vocabulary, an entire book may not be accessible to all students, but those who have specific interests will soon be reading parts of it. Considerable content knowledge can also be gained through the pictures. Dinosaur books are a particular favorite.

 Partner reading involves two students in the same rotating group. The pair chooses a book, then one partner can read to the other, partners can share reading every other page, or they can choral read together. Another variation is for each student to choose a book and read that choice to a partner. Many students have a favorite book and will reread and reread it until they are perfectly fluent.

 The *listening center* can be an additional stop. Here, students use headphones to read along with a book on tape. Multiple copies of each book should be available and all the components should be stored together in a baggie. The books may be those that students can read by themselves or nearly by themselves, or they may be classic children's read-alouds or content books. Tapes can be purchased or recorded by school personnel or volunteers. The librarian is an experienced storyteller and can always be counted on to record some of her favorite stories.

 Since primary rooms are filled with labels, word walls, and charts, *reading around the room* is an easy activity. Old language experience stories or samples of shared writing are usually posted or hanging on big stands. Yesterday's word study lesson might be left on the pocket chart, and students can work through all of the words again. With a magic pointer, preferably one without a sharp end, indvidual students or partners can read everything in the room.

If the *writing center* is scheduled immediately after the guided reading group, the writing activity can be an extension to the story and the teacher can provide directions before the students leave the group. Younger readers might label pictures, and older readers might retell the story. Students might have free choice about what to write on some days, but providing an activity idea usually works better. Monday morning is always a good time for relating weekend activities, and any time is a good time for writing a story. Students can make regular entries in writing journals and store them in the writing center. Making alphabet books is another favorite activity. Students can also write lists, copy classmates' names, or write letters.

 *Word study activities* can be set up on the pocket chart or in baggies on a table. For independent practice, teachers can ask students to repeat an activity that was already done with the whole class or in a small group. Flash cards, words related to the day's story, words to sort by beginning or ending sounds, words to sort by vowel sounds, concentration games, go fish games, making words, rhyming words, or category words are all good possibilities. Key features to making these activities go smoothly are making sure the students know how to do the activity independently, teaching the students to put the pieces back in the right bag, and not having too many activities available at one time. Teachers can color code activity pieces by running different colored markers over the backs and labeling the bags in the same colors. If the pieces are made of durable tagboard and laminated, they can withstand many years of use by little hands.

 Another activity center, the *poetry center,* can be stocked with poetry, patterned books, or nursery rhymes. This corner can also include poems the class has read or written. Students can read the poems or write their own illustrated personal copies.

 An *art center* is another option, especially if the project is an extension of the book. If students finish their independent reading tasks, the art center is the place they can visit until the last reading group is finished and whole-class activities resume.

On some days, free choice of any activity can be scheduled into the activity list and posted on the board as "Your Choice."

Using Miscue Inventories and Running Records

As mentioned earlier, at the end of each guided reading group session, one student stays, and the teacher takes a running record. Running records are similar to the miscue inventory (Goodman and Burke 1972). Running records and miscue inventories use responses that deviate from the text to gain insight into the processes the reader is using.

Miscue Inventory

A miscue inventory is more formal than a running record. A student's reading is taped, responses are recorded and coded according to comprehension patterns and grammatical relationship patterns, and the results are recorded on a reader profile chart. After reading, the student retells the story and that score is added to the other comprehension and grammatical pattern scores. When doing a miscue inventory, the teacher provides no aid to the student during reading. The recorded miscues include substitutions, omissions, insertions, reversals of words, repetitions, unsuccessful attempts, and partial attempts. By analyzing the miscues, the teacher determines which cueing systems the student is using and can also note whether the changes interrupt constructing meaning.

Running Records

The running record is not as formal as the miscue inventory, but the purpose is the same. Teachers use running records to document the first-time reading of a passage by a student. Teachers mark the text to indicate exactly how the student read the passage. They can analyze the errors to determine which cueing systems the student used and to find out whether the reader tried a second cueing system if the first one failed. If the student is using sound-symbol relationships (graphophonemic cues), the teacher might hear the student sounding out an unfamiliar word. If the reader uses sentence patterns (syntactic cues), she might substitute an incorrect word but one that fits grammatically within the sentence. If the student uses semantic cues, he might substitute an incorrect word that is consistent with the context of the story. Rapid correct reading usually means that the student knows the words as sight words, either those learned as a whole unit or those that have been practiced or analyzed so many times that they are instantly recognized. Although it is not a part of the formal marking system, teachers can determine when a student is using picture cues. The teacher will either see the student looking back and forth between the picture and the text or hear the student "read" something that is described through the picture but is not actually in the text.

When the reader understands a difficult word after examining it, she will often repeat the entire phrase that accompanies the word. An error such as this signals a reader who constructs meaning in entire expressive phrases. Errors or miscues that change the meaning of the text are the most serious. During the analysis of the running record, teachers should distinguish between those errors or miscues that were self-corrections, errors or miscues that did not interrupt comprehension, and errors or miscues that changed meaning. The most serious errors indicate that the student has used some cueing system but failed to monitor meaning. The reader is missing the main point. The text is supposed to make sense.

> **Serious errors show that the student is not reading for making sense.**

After the student has finished reading, the teacher asks some comprehension questions to make sure that the student understood the passage. Finally, the teacher calculates the percentage of words read correctly to establish if the material was at the independent level (99 to 100 percent), the instructional level (91 to 98 percent), or the frustrational level (90 percent or below). Many teachers also calculate the percentage of words read correctly and add in words that were self-corrected or words that were miscues but did not affect the meaning. If the student is at the independent level, it may be time to move the student to more difficult texts. Teachers use the information gleaned from running records to determine instruction and placement. A marking system for running records is presented in the next section with samples.

Teachers can use whatever the students are reading to take a running record, but sometimes a teacher reserves a book at a particular level just for running records or making initial assessments. These reserved books are called benchmark books (Fawson and Reutzel 2000). A benchmark book is not read with the entire group. Teachers can type up a benchmark piece and use it for several students. They can also compare the strategies several students used on that piece to determine what should be studied next.

Marking System

Although the marking system is relatively simple, teachers often use a tape recorder until the system becomes habitual, and they can mark as fast as the student can read. The following system uses a combination of markings used in running records and in the miscue inventory. Teachers can make checks on a blank sheet of paper for every word read correctly, but using a duplicated copy of the text is much easier (Tompkins 1997).

The following errors or miscues are marked:

◆ substitutions   ◆ insertions

◆ provided words   ◆ repetitions

◆ omissions   ◆ self-corrections

SUBSTITUTIONS Students often make several partial or whole word attempts at a difficult word. All attempts can be recorded by placing hyphens between each attempt so teachers can later recall that all were attempts for the same word. When a reader substitutes an incorrect word, substitutions are recorded by placing the substituted word above the correct word in the text.

This will

◆ That's what I'll do this morning.

Student read:
"This will I'll do this morning."

Th-This-That

◆ That's what I'll do this morning.

Student read:
"Th-This-That what I'll do this morning."

PROVIDED WORDS Often a student makes several attempts but is unable to successfully identify a word and appeals to the teacher to provide the word. Teachers should not provide words or correct unsuccessful attempts unless the student asks, verbally or nonverbally, for the correct word. A dead stop followed by a long pause usually indicates that the reader would like to have the word provided. Urge the student to identify the word before providing it. If the reader makes no attempt, provide the word so the student is able to make sense out of the rest of the story. Record a P above the word that you provided. Record the attempts as substitutions and place a P after the last unsuccessful substitution.

> P
> ◆ His name was ~~Antonio~~.
>
> Student read: "His name was . . ."

> Anton–Anthony–P
> ◆ His name was Antonio.
>
> Student read: "His name was Anton, Anthony . . ."

OMISSIONS Omissions are words that the reader left out. Sometimes students omit whole words and sometimes just an ending or a syllable. Record omissions by drawing a line through the omitted word or the omitted part of the word.

> ◆ He parked the car in the ~~small~~ garage.
>
> Student read: "He parked the car in the garage."

> ◆ He park~~ed~~ the car in the small garage.
>
> Student read: "He park the car in the small garage."

INSERTIONS Insertions are words the student adds that do not appear in the text. Insertions are marked with a caret sign where the insertion was made.

◆ He went very fast on his ˄ scooter.
  little

   Student read: "He went very fast on his little scooter."

REPETITIONS Repetitions occur for a number of different reasons. Sometimes readers stop in anticipation of identifying the next word. They then reread the previous word and continue, especially if the first repeated word is part of a phrase. Upon reading the sentence further, readers may realize that they have misread something and go back to correct it, rereading part or all of the sentence. (Marking self-corrections is discussed next.) Sometimes readers realize that their intonation was incorrect when they see the end punctuation and reread the sentence with the correct intonation. With repetition, some readers may even substitute an incorrect word for the correct one, even though they read the word correctly the first time. Repetitions should be marked with an underline. If the reader repeats a single word, draw the line under the word. If the student repeats a whole phrase or a partial phrase, draw a line under the whole phrase. If student repeats the word or phrase more than once, draw a double line.

◆ She sat in the <u>old</u> rocking chair.

   Student read: "She sat in the old old rocking chair."

◆ <u>There was</u> a loud noise.

   Student read: "There was there was a loud noise."

◆ <u>With a</u> thunderous crash, the chair split in two.

   Student read: "With a with a with a thunderous crash, the chair split in two."

SELF-CORRECTIONS Self-corrections can follow substitutions or may be part of a repeated phrase. Use SC to designate a self-correction. It is not necessary to write the correct word. When the self-correction is tied in with a repetition, it is helpful to underline the repetition with an SC to note which word was self-corrected during the repetition. When the student goes back and forth making several attempts, self-correcting and repeating, it gets a little difficult to mark. Noting the strategies the reader used is much more important than absolutely perfect marking.

wind SC
◆ I like to look out the window at noon.

wind
Student read: "I like to look out the ∧ [with a long i] window at noon."

wind SC
◆ I like to <u>look out the</u> window at noon.

Student read: "I like to look out the wind, window, look out the window at noon."

After recording students' miscues or errors, teachers must also ask questions to ensure students' comprehension. A simple line of questioning has students retell the story. The teacher may also ask for students' opinions. Some examples follow:

◆ What was the story about?

◆ Who was the main character?

◆ What happened at the end of the story?

◆ Did you like the story? Why? (or Why not?)

◆ What did you think was going to happen?

◆ What would you change about the story?

◆ What is your favorite part of the story?

Marking System Samples

Figures 3.8 and 3.9 are samples of marked running records of two readers, Lucy and Larry, and illustrate how much teachers can learn from running records. The teacher typed the story on a sheet of paper to use for each student's running record. The students were then introduced to the story and made predictions from the cover, which contained the title and a picture of a sleeping cat. They were given the words to the title, *Lazy Cat.*

Lucy's Sample

When Lucy read this story, it was obvious from the markings that she used several strategies. Other strategies used can only be ascertained by the expression in her voice and on her face. Lucy expected the story to make sense and read with great expression when she understood the meaning. When she substituted *cattle* for *children,* she knew that cattle had no place in the story and appealed for the word. She continued with other words that might match *pass by* such as *please by,* which did not work, then *play,* then *pals,* and when she was provided with *pass,* she repeated *pass by.* At other times, she was willing to accept something that almost made sense: *This will all [SC] I'll do this morning* or *See where it fall.*

Lucy used beginning and ending sounds but did not pay close attention to the order of letters or did not know the vowel sounds, substituting *ball* for *bell, fall* for *fell, with* for *white, lit* for *lot* and *his* for *has.* Her eyes occasionally traveled back and forth on a line, and once in a while she made some odd connections. In *and then maybe play tug,* she read *and then be play too mar again today.* She went back to pick up *may,* connected some other letters, realized that none of it connected, decided it was incomprehensible, and just went on.

Lucy was able to retell most of what the cat did and read the repeating lines with greater expression each time. She read 156 out of 182 words correctly to total 86 percent correct. If the self-corrections are not counted, she read 90 percent correctly, putting this story just within her frustrational range. The story offers several possibilities for instruction for Lucy.

Lazy Cat (read by Lucy)

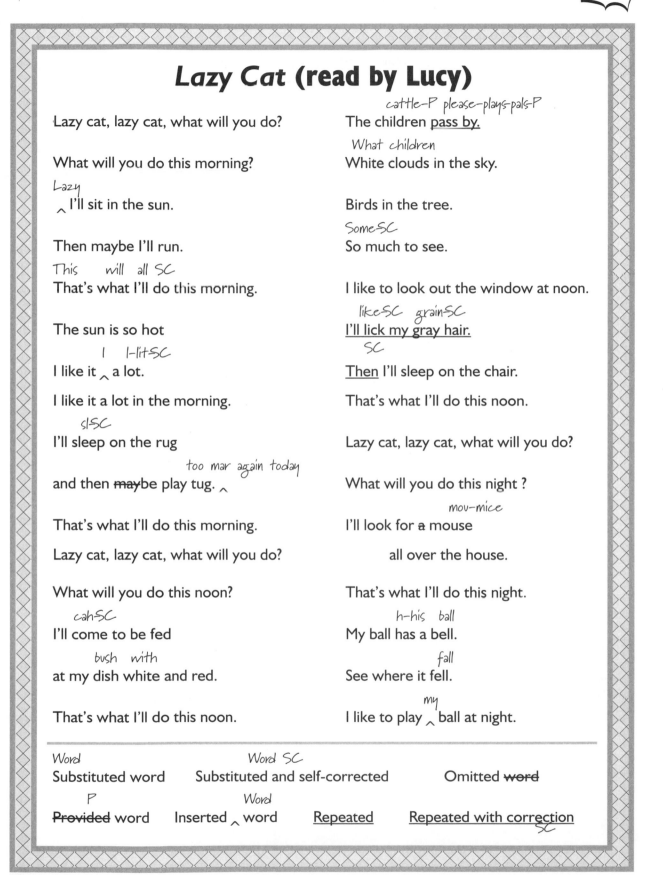

Lazy cat, lazy cat, what will you do?

What will you do this morning?

Lazy
^ I'll sit in the sun.

Then maybe I'll run.

This   will   all SC
That's what I'll do this morning.

The sun is so hot
       I   l–lit SC
I like it ^ a lot.

I like it a lot in the morning.

      sl SC
I'll sleep on the rug

                    too mar again today
and then ~~may~~be play tug. ^

That's what I'll do this morning.

Lazy cat, lazy cat, what will you do?

What will you do this noon?

     cah SC
I'll come to be fed

        bush   with
at my dish white and red.

That's what I'll do this noon.

                cattle–P please–plays–pals–P
The children <u>pass by.</u>

 What children
White clouds in the sky.

Birds in the tree.

Some SC
So much to see.

I like to look out the window at noon.

      like SC   grain SC
<u>I'll lick my gray hair.</u>

        SC
<u>Then</u> I'll sleep on the chair.

That's what I'll do this noon.

Lazy cat, lazy cat, what will you do?

What will you do this night ?

                mov–mice
I'll look for ~~a~~ mouse

        all over the house.

That's what I'll do this night.

          h–his   ball
My ball has a bell.

                fall
See where it fell.

          my
I like to play ^ ball at night.

Word
Substituted word

Word SC
Substituted and self-corrected

Omitted ~~word~~

P
~~Provided~~ word

Word
Inserted ^ word

<u>Repeated</u>

<u>Repeated with correction</u>
              SC

Figure 3.8

SkyLight Professional Development

Larry's Sample

Larry was more particular. Sentences had to sound just right. When he read *That's what I'll do the morning,* he immediately changed it to *this morning.* When he omitted *a* in *I like it a lot,* he noticed the structure and repeated the sentence correctly. Other substitutions had acceptable structure so he did not notice, for example, *Then children pass by* and *white clouds in the skies.* He even got the more difficult vowel combinations and figured out *clouds* with */cl/-/ow/-clouds.*

Larry used semantic cues (the sense of the story), syntactic cues (the sentence structure), and graphophonemic cues. He was able to retell most of the story. He read 168 out of 182 words correctly, totaling 92 percent correct. If the self-corrections and miscues that did not affect the meaning are not counted, he read 98 percent correctly. Larry can move up to a story at the next level, where he will have more problem-solving opportunities.

TEACHER QUOTE

" Guided reading is an excellent way to meet the diverse needs of readers. It is structured to teach skills to different students, depending on their needs. Guided reading is a framework that allows the flexibility needed to differentiate instruction in order to meet the unique needs of all students. "

—Jill VanDerveer
1st grade teacher
Robert Crown School, Wauconda, IL

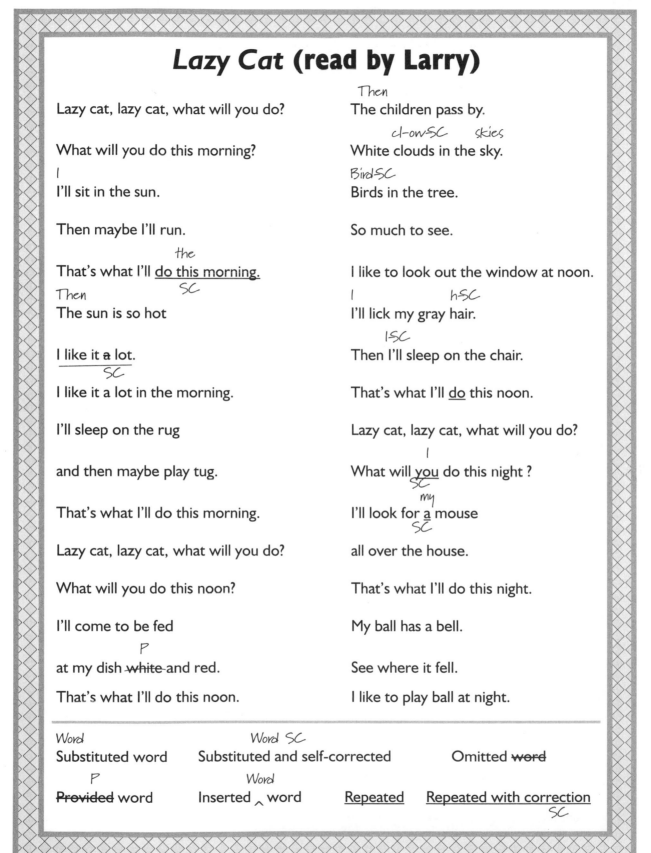

Lazy Cat (read by Larry)

Lazy cat, lazy cat, what will you do?

What will you do this morning?
I
I'll sit in the sun.

Then maybe I'll run.
                    the
That's what I'll <u>do this morning.</u>
Then   *SC*
The sun is so hot

I like it ~~a~~ lot.
         SC
I like it a lot in the morning.

I'll sleep on the rug

and then maybe play tug.

That's what I'll do this morning.

Lazy cat, lazy cat, what will you do?

What will you do this noon?

I'll come to be fed
              P
at my dish ~~white~~ and red.

That's what I'll do this noon.

Then
The children pass by.
     cl–owSC   *skies*
White clouds in the sky.
BirdSC
Birds in the tree.

So much to see.

I like to look out the window at noon.
I   *hSC*
I'll lick my gray hair.
              ISC
Then I'll sleep on the chair.

That's what I'll <u>do</u> this noon.

Lazy cat, lazy cat, what will you do?
                    I
What will <u>you</u> do this night ?
          SC
          my
I'll look for <u>a</u> mouse
          SC
all over the house.

That's what I'll do this night.

My ball has a bell.

See where it fell.

I like to play ball at night.

Word
Substituted word

Word SC
Substituted and self-corrected

Omitted ~~word~~

P
~~Provided~~ word

Word
Inserted ∧ word

<u>Repeated</u>

<u>Repeated with correction</u>
                    SC

Figure 3.9

Steps for Taking a Running Record

1 With the running record chart in front of you, have the student sit where you can easily see the text as she reads.

2 Briefly introduce the story and have the student discuss the cover and make predictions on what the story will be about.

3 Record how the student reads each word using the marking system described earlier and provided here. (It may be easier to type or write the story into the chart before taking the running record. As you become more familiar with taking running records, you will be able to use the marking system without the entire story present on the running record chart.) Record each word as it appears in the book, starting a new line when a new line appears in the student's book. Be sure to record the page number each line appears on so you can go back if necessary.

4 Self-corrections are not recorded as errors. Record errors and self-corrections with tick marks in the appropriate columns, then note which cueing systems the student's used when the error was made and when the student self-corrected. Use the codes provided here.

5 When you are finished, tally the errors and write the total in the appropriate boxes. Remember, do not count self-corrections as errors.

Taking a Running Record

Running records can be used in any format. Teachers can type the passage or story on a separate piece of paper and then mark how students read. Teachers who are familiar with taking running records may simply use the marking system described previously on a blank piece of paper and analyze the student's progress from the markings. However, more information can be derived from a running record. This is shown in the simple running record format that appears in Figure 3.10 as a sample. (See the blackline masters at the end of the chapter for a blank running record.) Directions and tips are outlined to the left and below.

Marking System for Running Records

Use the following marking system to record how the student reads each word.

✓	P
Read correctly	~~Provided~~ word
Word	*Word* / SC
Substituted word	Substituted and self-corrected
	Word
Omitted ~~word~~	Inserted ˄ word
<u>Repeated</u>	<u>Repeated with correction</u> SC

Cues Used

Semantic—Meaning (M)

Syntactic—Structure of language (S)

Visual—Graphophonemic/orthographic (V)

Schematic—Personal background (P)

Sample Running Record

Student's name: _Chris_   Date _9/20_

Page	Title: Brown Bunny	E	SC	E	SC
		Totals:		Cues	Used
		E	SC	E	SC
1	✓ ✓ hoped|SC ✓ ✓ ✓ Brown Bunny hopped to the park.		1	Ⓜ Ⓢ Ⓟ P	Ⓜ Ⓢ V P
3	✓ ✓ on ✓ ✓ He hopped under the trees.	1		Ⓜ Ⓢ V P	
6	✓ ✓ ✓ follow|SC He stopped near the flowers ✓ ✓ ✓ ✓ to say hello to the bees.	1	1	Ⓜ Ⓢ V P	M Ⓢ Ⓥ P
9	✓ ✓ ✓ ✓ Brown Bunny hopped all day on–in|SC ✓ ✓ until it was dark.	1	1	M Ⓢ V P	M Ⓢ Ⓥ P
12	✓ ✓ say|SC ✓ ✓ Then he saw he was alone ✓ ✓ ✓ ✓ ✓ ✓ and he hopped home from the park.		1	Ⓜ Ⓢ V P Ⓜ Ⓢ V P	Ⓜ Ⓢ Ⓟ P
	Totals:	3	4	6|5|1|0	2|2|3|1

Scoring:

Running Words / Errors $\dfrac{44}{3}$ $=14.6$ **Error Ratio =** 1:15

$\dfrac{\text{(Running Words – Errors)}}{\text{Running Words}} \times 100$ $\dfrac{(44-5)}{44} \times 100$ **Reading Level =** 93%

❏ Independent 99–100   ✗ Instructional 91–98%   ❏ Frustrational 90% or below

$\dfrac{\text{(E + SC)}}{\text{SC}}$ $\dfrac{3+4}{4}$ **Self-Correction Ratio =** 1:2

Analysis of Cues Used: Relied on visual cues when stumped; flipped back and forth to look at the illustrations. Better use of semantic cues — getting the idea. Much better level of monitoring here than last time!

Figure 3.10

Scoring a Running Record

Error Ratio

To calculate the error ratio, use the total of running words (words the student read in the story) divided by the total errors the student made. Always round up to the nearest whole number.

$$\frac{\text{Running Words}}{\text{Error(s)}} = \text{Error Rate}$$

For example, if there were 100 words in the story, and the student made 12 errors:

$$\frac{100}{12} = 9$$

The error ratio is 1:9 which means for every word read incorrectly, 11 words were read correctly.

Reading Level

To calculate the student's reading level, subtract the total errors from the total of running words, then divide the remainder by the running words. Multiply the resulting number by 100.

$$\frac{\text{(Running Words} - \text{Errors)}}{\text{Running Words}} \times 100 = \underline{\qquad}\%$$

For example, using the above numbers of 12 errors and 100 running words:

$$\frac{(100 - 12)}{100} \times 100 = 88\% \qquad \text{OR} \qquad \frac{(100 - 12)}{100} = \frac{88}{100} \times 100 = 88\%$$

Levels of Reading: ◆ Independent = 99–100%
　　　　　　　　　◆ Instructional = 91–98%
　　　　　　　　　◆ Frustrational = 80% or below

Self-Correction Ratio

The self-correction ratio works the same way as the error ratio—it expresses how many words the student corrected compared to how many errors. Calculating the self-correction rate is an important step because it helps determine if the student is self-monitoring his or her own reading. The self-correction ratio is calculated by adding the total errors to the total self-corrections, then dividing the sum by the total self-corrections.

$$\frac{(E + SC)}{SC} = \text{Self-Correction Rate}$$

For example, with a total of 12 errors and 6 self-corrections:

$$\frac{(12 + 6)}{6} = 3 \qquad \text{OR} \qquad \frac{(18)}{6} = 3$$

The self-correction rate is 1:3. This means that the student is correcting one out of every three errors. A ratio of 1:4 or less means that the student is self-monitoring.

Analysis of Cues Used

There are no calculations for this section of the running record. It includes only teacher observation and analysis. Total each of the cueing systems the student used for errors and self-corrections. If only one cue was used, then you know the student needs more instruction on other cues. If, for example, you notice that only visual cues are used, then you know the student relies heavily on illustrations and you can design instruction from there. An even or nearly even distribution of cues used demonstrates that the student is comfortable using all of the systems. Students may be ignoring cues when they make an error, or they may be misusing cues.

Chapter Three Summary

Guided reading is a highly useful instructional strategy at the primary level. The procedures are familiar to primary teachers. The continuing diagnostic and prescriptive features help place students at a level where they can be successful, yet stretch to learn new skills. What guided reading provides, most of all, is an opportunity to learn comprehension within the context of reading whole text.

TEACHER QUOTE

> " By incorporating learning stations into your guided reading sessions, all students are engaged in meaningful literacy activities at the same time. Guided reading is a wonderful way to incorporate a variety of learning experiences for students. "
>
> —Jill VanDerveer
> 1st grade teacher
> Robert Crown School, Wauconda, IL

Chapter 3 Blackline Masters

◆ Independent Activities Icons

- Guided Reading
- Independent Reading
- Partner Reading
- Listening Center
- Reading Around the Room

- Writing Center
- Word Study Activities
- Poetry Center
- Art Center

◆ Running Record

◆ Behavior Checklist for Primary Students

◆ Ideas for Classroom Use

- Make overhead transparencies or posters of each icon. Explain each type of activity or center to students as you display each icon.
- Create a daily agenda board. Place the Independent Activities Icons beneath appropriate student groups.
- Photocopy and use the Running Record blackline master as a tool for assessing students' reading, especially when conducting individual running record sessions.
- The Behavior Checklist for Primary Students may be used either with guided reading groups or with individual students.

Guided Reading

Independent Reading

Partner Reading

Listening Center

Reading Around the Room

Writing Center

Word Study Activities

Art Center

Running Record

Student's name:_____   Date _____

Page	Title: _____	Totals:		Cues	Used
		E	SC	E	SC
	Totals:				

Scoring:

<u>Running Words</u>   _____   **Error Ratio =**
    Errors

<u>(Running Words – Errors)</u> x 100   _____ x 100   **Reading Level =**
    Running Words

❑ Independent 99–100%   ❑ Instructional 91–98%   ❑ Frustrational 90% or below

<u>(E + SC)</u>   _____   **Self-Correction Ratio =**
    SC

Analysis of Cues Used:

Behavior Checklist for Primary Students

(Circle the appropriate number.)

Focus

Involved in assignment				Off task
5	4	3	2	I

Head and Body Movement

Limited movement				Much movement
5	4	3	2	I
Feet still				Tapping
5	4	3	2	I
Comfortable				Slouching, wiggling
5	4	3	2	I

Facial Expression

Involved, interested				Frustrated, bored
5	4	3	2	I
Shows emotion appropriate to content				Emotionless
5	4	3	2	I

Eyes

Left-to-right sweep				All over page
5	4	3	2	I
Checks picture/text				Skips picture/skips text
5	4	3	2	I

Lips

Reads silently		Mouths words		Letter by letter sounds
5	4	3	2	I

Hands

Holds book at appropriate distance			Distance indicates vision problem	
5	4	3	2	I
Finger points in sweeps across page		Finger points word by word	Frames word with fingers	
5	4	3	2	I

Speed of Completion

Fast				Slow
5	4	3	2	I

ADAPTED FROM PRIMARY OBSERVATION CHECKLIST DEVELOPED BY PATSY CLARK.

Guided Reading in Grades 3–12

Light is the task when many share the toil.

—HOMER, The *ILIAD*

Guided reading in the intermediate, middle, and upper grades is handled a little differently than guided reading in the primary grades, but it accomplishes all of the same purposes. Guided reading allows teachers to provide guidance and support while students are reading. During guided reading, the teacher and students read silently and then talk, think, and question their way through a book. The teacher shows the students what questions to ask themselves as readers and what to ask of the text so that each student can discover the author's meaning on the first reading (Mooney 1990). Guided reading models what expert readers do when reading independently.

79

As students conquer word recognition, comprehension strategies take the forefront. This proves to be difficult for many intermediate and middle graders who have carried over only limited strategies from the primary grades. Primary texts are written with simple, straightforward story lines. This is done purposely, because so much of readers' cognitive energy is spent on decoding words and learning basic skills that they do not have much energy left for a complex story line. Generally, if readers can say the words in a first-grade text, they can comprehend the story. However, intermediate-, middle-, and upper-grade texts contain a greater variety of text structures, more subtle meanings, increased vocabulary, more complex sentence structure, and content that ranges further from the reader's direct experiences. Students in the intermediate, middle, and upper grades need direct instruction in comprehension strategies with significant opportunities to apply them in guided circumstances. Reading instruction often continues into high school as students encounter increasingly difficult text and need to alter their strategies to comprehend complex text. Even accomplished high school readers benefit from guided reading as they learn which strategies to apply to specialized text.

The guided reading process in grades 3–12 is slightly different than the primary format. In the advanced version, there are key elements to a guided reading lesson (see Figure 4.1).

Choosing Short Passages

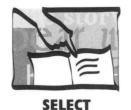

SELECT

The teacher divides a story or novel into short passages based on the action of the story, stopping in meaningful places rather than just at the bottom of a page. This is referred to as text segmenting. Decisions about segmenting should be based on the text content and the ideas and information presented, not on where the page or paragraph ends (Beck et al. 1998). For readers who are having the most difficulty, short may mean just one paragraph. For readers who can handle the text rather well, short may mean two or three pages. Teachers segment the text into shorter passages for several reasons. Students can keep the content in mind more easily; it is easier to find, prove, and

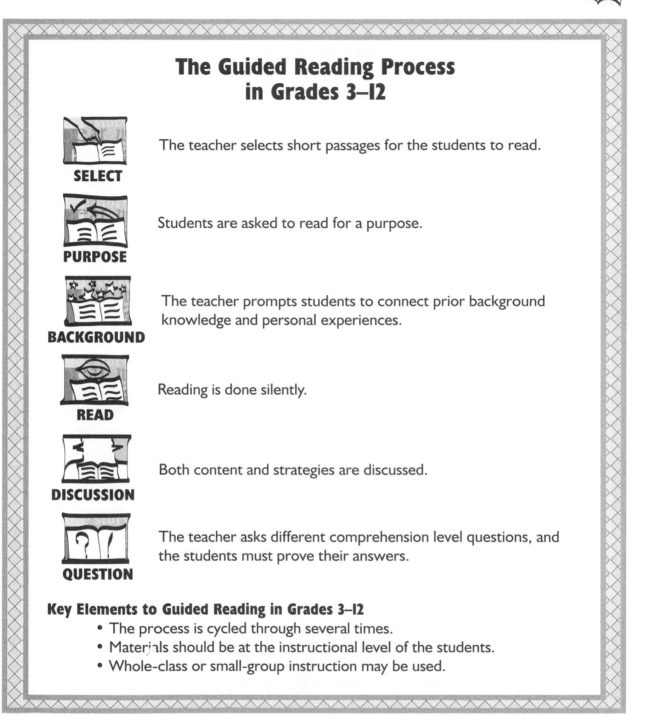

The Guided Reading Process in Grades 3–12

SELECT

The teacher selects short passages for the students to read.

PURPOSE

Students are asked to read for a purpose.

BACKGROUND

The teacher prompts students to connect prior background knowledge and personal experiences.

READ

Reading is done silently.

DISCUSSION

Both content and strategies are discussed.

QUESTION

The teacher asks different comprehension level questions, and the students must prove their answers.

Key Elements to Guided Reading in Grades 3–12
- The process is cycled through several times.
- Materials should be at the instructional level of the students.
- Whole-class or small-group instruction may be used.

Figure 4.1

discuss answers; and shorter segments are not as daunting to struggling readers as reading the whole story or chapter is. Dividing text into smaller segments is crucial for struggling readers and students with limited English proficiency who may give up during a difficult passage and pay little attention to the rest of the selection.

Breaking the selection into smaller parts is certainly preferable to the traditional pattern of reading the whole selection and asking questions at the end. In the traditional framework, students often had problems while they were reading but had no strategies for solving them; some students simply finished the text knowing they were lost but not knowing why (Beck et al. 1998). Discussion that occurs at the end, even though it might analyze a particular part of the story, does little to help students clarify the entire story when they have carried some misconception or fuzzy idea throughout the entire piece. Discussion at the end is seldom little more than assessment.

> **Even accomplished high school readers benefit from guided reading as they learn which strategies to apply to specialized text.**

When the class takes on the story a little at a time, they unravel the content, clear up misconceptions, and make connections. Since characters and setting are introduced at the beginning of a story or a novel, stopping for discussion is especially important so readers are not confused throughout the selection. A critical spot for clarification and discussion is when the main problem of the story is revealed by the author. Stopping for discussion at this point helps students understand exactly what dilemma the characters face. When a section is clarified through discussion and questioning, the chances that the reader will be able to better connect that content to the following sections increases.

Breaking text into smaller segments also fosters good modeling. Middle school teachers who were trained in intermediate and primary reading techniques learned to read and question, read and question from the basals. This is what the teachers' manual said to do. Furthermore, dividing the text into smaller segments is what independent readers do. They read and then stop to consider, connect, or consolidate. It may not seem so to expert adult readers because they can do so much of it simultaneously. Most teachers can remember reading something that triggered an idea for a reading lesson, minutes later finding the book open in their laps with the realization that they had stopped reading long ago. Unfortunately, I sometimes consider while I continue reading and have no idea of what I just read.

The teacher can monitor and provide immediate support for the entire process more efficiently when guided reading is done in shorter sections. Students who were trying to monitor their comprehension can find out if they were on track. Teachers can stop and send students who were not monitoring their comprehension back to the beginning of the segment before it is too late. Fix-ups are done on the spot. The readers do not continue with vague notions, unable to connect ideas.

Setting a Purpose for Silent Reading

PURPOSE

Before students begin reading silently, the teacher sets a purpose for reading by asking a question or asking for a prediction. This gives readers something to look for instead of not knowing what to pay attention to and then reading passively. It also allows sufficient time for students to formulate a thoughtful answer instead of the second or so that some teachers wait before calling on the first student who raised his or her hand. Having time to process what has been read also increases active participation and engagement, especially for inclusion students. Slow or struggling readers can be successful as they search for and find a particular piece of information even if they do not understand all the nuances until the discussion occurs.

Connecting Prior Background Knowledge

BACKGROUND

The teacher may want to provide students with information on new concepts, review previously taught reading strategies, or introduce new strategies. With the appropriate information, students can connect prior background knowledge and personal experiences to what they read.

Discussing Content and Strategies

DISCUSSION

After the students have read the passage silently, the teacher repeats the purpose-setting question and the class discusses various parts of the text. This discussion accomplishes two things, sometimes simultaneously. First, the discussion helps students clear up any misconceptions or confusion about what was read. Second, the discussion guides students to the reading strategies they used or need to use and leads students to experience different levels of comprehension, not just the basic content of the passage. In the guided reading discussion, teachers' questions must focus both on the content and on the reading strategies. They may be strategies teachers know their students need or strategies required to read challenging text. It is very important that both the content and strategies used to comprehend the passage are part of the discussion. If they are not both included, it becomes just a question-and-answer session about the content or a direct reading skills instruction lesson. Refer back to the checklist in chapter 1 that lists both reader characteristics and text characteristics to consider when formulating questions.

QUESTION

The discussion usually leads seamlessly into questioning. Of course, the content questions are the usual who, what, when, where, why, and how, but the forever-present reading strategy question is: "How did you know that?" Students answer that question by finding the relevant sentences, telling what clues they used to draw a conclusion or make an inference, laying out several actions that were part of a related sequence, or referring back to the cause. Sometimes the answer to "How did you know that?" is from prior experience, another class, a previously read book, or something that happened outside of school. The answer might also be "I just saw it in my head and knew what it looked like." The teacher should name the strategies as students report them—relating prior knowledge, inferring, visualizing, etc.—so students consciously learn them by name. The idea is to make the strategies a conscious part of the students' repertoires (Mooney 1995b).

The teacher or students should also explain how they used each strategy in the current situation. Following are some examples:

◆ "I knew that was what the first section talked about so I went back and found it in the text."

◆ "I thought about how I would feel if I were in the jam he was in."

◆ "I did not know what that word meant, but from the sentence, I figured out it had to be some part on the ship."

This helps make thinking visible in the mind of a student who may have used the strategy intuitively. It also clarifies the process for other students who had no idea how to make sense of the text. Many struggling students assume others just know the answer because they are smart rather than realizing that they used some technique to figure it out. If no one knows how to solve the problem, the teacher should model the strategy and think aloud while going through the steps she used to decipher the text.

In addition to content questions and comprehension strategy questions, a third class of questioning focuses on fix-up strategies. When something goes wrong, and the text does not make sense, readers need to know how to fix it rather than just blindly going on. Using fix-up strategies is also a comprehension strategy, but fix-up questions do not always fit as easily into the flow of the discussion. Opportunities to discuss fix-up strategies usually occur in unplanned circumstances. Teachers can model fix-up strategies such as rereading, rethinking, looking for alternatives, skipping, reading on to look for clarification, or asking for help during guided reading. Expert readers are better at monitoring their comprehension and knowing what to do if the text does not make sense. Both of these skills can be taught during guided reading.

If students volunteer answers that are off base, ask them what gave them those ideas. The answers can be very revealing. After reading a book that described the beach after a hurricane, I asked for a description of the aftermath. One student said there were ribbons on the beach. Upon further questioning, she found the passage that she had remembered. It said that the wind blew whirling ribbons of sand into the air. She needed a fix-up strategy when what she read did not seem likely.

Choosing Instructional-Level Material and Grouping Students

Text should be at the students' instructional level—easy enough that it can be read but difficult enough that it provides some challenges in comprehension or in content. In grades 3–12, a broader range in reading ability can be accommodated in a guided reading lesson, because students receive significant support at several stopping points. Students who would be lost gain clarification during the discussion and are ready to tackle the next section with greater understanding.

In grades 3–12, it is possible to do whole-class lessons during guided reading, although the teacher must be careful to involve all the students. Smaller groups may still be utilized for specific instruction. Guided reading is just one part of the reading program; it is the application with guidance. Instruction must still include word study, direct instruction, independent reading, reader response in written and project form, reading instruction for expository materials, and an abundant amount of writing connected to reading.

A Sample Guided Reading Lesson

In this lesson, sixth-grade students were reading a passage from the Robert Louis Stevenson classic, *Treasure Island* (1939). The teacher wanted to be sure that the students noticed the foreshadowing of a major problem in the story: the deception of Squire Trelawney by Long John Silver. The clues were subtle for eleven-year-old readers, so the teacher focused the purpose-setting question on that foreshadowing. She then addressed a few other issues that could be obstacles to comprehension.

So far, students knew the following: Squire Trelawney, Dr. Livesey, and young Jim Hawkins were about to start a journey to retrieve the hidden treasure of the pirate Captain Flint. After Billy Bones, a guest at the Hawkins' inn, died from a fit of apoplexy (a stroke), Jim and his mother found a treasure map in Bones's sea chest. Before dying, Billy Bones had warned Jim to beware of a one-legged pirate, another member of Flint's crew, who was trying to find the treasure map. Squire Trelawney wrote a letter to Livesey from Bristol, where he was outfitting a ship for the voyage.

The teacher asked the students to read Squire Trelawney's letter to decide if they would trust him to be the leader of the expedition. This question set a purpose for reading and guided the students to be on the lookout for possible flaws in Trelawney's judgment. She also told the students that authors do not always directly write things that they wish the reader to know, so the reader has to be on the lookout for small clues. Authors do this to make it more interesting for readers as they discover events that all the characters may not yet know. Here is the letter the students read:

Dear Livesey,—As I do not know whether you are at the Hall or still in London, I send this in double to both places.

The ship is bought and fitted. She lies at anchor, ready for sea. You never imagined a sweeter schooner—a child might sail her—two hundred tons; name, Hispaniola.

I got her through my old friend, Blandly, who has proved himself throughout the most surprising trump. The admirable fellow literally slaved in my interest, and so, I may say, did everyone in Bristol, as soon as they got wind of the port we sailed for—treasure, I mean.

Blandley himself found the Hispaniola, and by the most admirable management got her for the merest trifle. There is a class of men in Bristol monstrously preju-diced against Blandly. They go the length of declaring that this honest creature would do anything for money, that the Hispaniola belonged to him, and that he sold to me absurdly high—the most transparent calumnies. None of them dare, however, to deny the merits of the ship.

So far there was not a hitch. The workpeople, to be sure—riggers and what not—were most annoyingly slow; but time cured that. It was the crew that troubled me.

I wished a round score of men—in case of natives, buccaneers, or the odious French—and I had the worry of the deuce itself to find so much as half a dozen, till the most remarkable stroke of fortune brought me the very man that I required.

I was standing on the dock, when, by the merest accident, I fell in talk with him. I found he was an old sailor, kept a public-house, knew all the seafaring men in Bristol, had lost his health ashore, and wanted a good berth as cook to get to sea again. He had hobbled down there that morning, he said, to get a smell of the salt.

I was monstrously touched—so would you have been—and, out of pure pity, I engaged him on the spot to be ship's cook. Long John Silver he is called, and has lost a leg; but that I regarded as a recommendation, since he lost it in his country's service, under immortal Hawke. He has no pension, Livesey. Imagine the abom-inable age we live in!

Well sir, I thought I had only found a cook, but it was a crew I had discovered. Between Silver and myself we got together in a few days a company of the tough-est old salts imaginable—not pretty to look at, but fellows, by their faces, of the most indomitable spirit. I declare we could fight a frigate.

Long John even got rid of two out of the six or seven I had already engaged. He showed me in a moment that they were just the sort of fresh-water swabs we had to fear in an adventure of importance.

I am in the most magnificent health and spirits, eating like a bull, sleeping like a tree, yet I shall not enjoy a moment till I hear my old tarpaulins tramping round the capstan. Seaward ho! Hang the treasure! It's the glory of the sea that has turned my head. So now, Livesey, come post; do not lose an hour, if you respect me.

Let young Hawkins go at once to see his mother, with Redruth for a guard; and then both come full speed to Bristol.

John Trelawney

EXCERPTED FROM *TREASURE ISLAND* (STEVENSON 1929).

The teacher then repeated the question "Would you trust Squire Trelawney to lead the expedition?" Some students responded that Trelawney may not have made a good deal when he bought the ship. The evidence is conflicting, since the squire claimed that he bought the ship for the merest trifle, that his friend and agent slaved in his interest, and that his friend is an honest creature. Others said that Blandly would do anything for money since he sold the ship at an absurdly high price and it actually belonged to him. The teacher highlighted that this was conflicting information and asked students how they could decide what was really happening. The conversation expanded to a discussion of what good readers do when they notice contradictory facts.

Some students noticed that it was an incredible coincidence that Long John Silver, "by the merest accident," was on the docks where the ship was being outfitted and had a long patriotic tale to tell Trelawney, who incidentally seemed unable to keep a secret. Students also questioned Trelawney's judgment when he hired Silver, a complete stranger, out of pity, and then permitted him to find the crew and fire two sailors that the squire had already hired. Some students decided that Trelawney's enthusiasm may have clouded his judgment. Some were quite suspicious when Long John "hobbled" to the dock to get a smell of salt air. Could he be the one-legged pirate that Jim Hawkins had been warned about? If the students had missed some of these subtleties, the teacher would have guided them to the clues with questions:

◆ Do you think the squire got a good deal on the ship?

◆ Was the squire lucky to meet Long John Silver?

◆ How is Long John described?

◆ Would you trust a complete stranger whom you met on the dock to hire your crew?

◆ How did you judge which of the statements were probably true?

Once the students understood that they should be wary of Long John's intentions, the teacher might have asked other questions that would have helped remove obstacles to the students' understanding, increased or activated their background knowledge, or made them consciously aware of the various strategies. Most of these questions would have probably been integrated with the previous discussion as various points were brought up. Not all of the following questions would be asked after just one passage, but they give an indication of the types of questions that could be used in a similar situation.

Q. Why did the squire want a score of men (twenty) for the crew of the ship?

A. He needed a full crew to protect against natives, buccaneers, and the odious French.

After students had cited this line, the teacher would ask them to explain its meaning and what they knew about these three groups of possible enemies.

Q. What does this list of enemies tell you about the times Jim lived in and about the destination of the ship?

A. The French and the English were enemies, pirates were a threat at sea, and they would be traveling outside European waters. The treasure map indicated the island was off Caracas.

If a student responded with one of these pieces of information, the teacher might have asked, "How did you know that?" so other students could have found out that their classmates were connecting social studies lessons to this book or had done outside reading. Successful students do not just know things—they connect information. If no one knows, the teacher should supply the information.

The teacher might ask students to describe Long John Silver, despite the fact that there is no description in the passage. Readers learn that they should be visualizing and filling in details that the author has left out. Visual images last longer than verbal descriptions and help students remember the story.

Vocabulary can be addressed during the discussion so that lack of word knowledge does not inhibit meaning. *Old salts, merest trifle, hobbled, engaged,* and *swabs* are important to the story. The teacher can model how to use the strategy of context clues by asking, "Even if you did not know what old salts were, when you read 'we got together in a few days a company of the toughest old salts imaginable,' what words did you put in their place? What words would make sense in that passage?"

At this point, the teacher might ask a student to summarize the passage or ask students to pick out critical ideas and less relevant details. Process questions—such as "Why is that point critical to the story?" or "What detail can be left out without making a difference?"—help students learn to differentiate between main ideas and irrelevant details. The teacher can then ask the students to predict what might happen on the journey so they can practice their inferential skills, have their interests piqued, and discover a new purpose for reading. See Figure 4.2 for questions that might be asked to promote practice with the different reading strategies. See the end of this chapter for a blank blackline master of a Guided Reading Questions Planner for Promoting Reading Strategies. (See Figure 1.2 in chapter 1 for a comprehensive list of reading comprehension strategies.)

Sample Guided Reading Questions Planner for Promoting Reading Strategies for *Treasure Island*

Connecting Prior Background
- What does this list of enemies tell you about the times Jim lived in and about the destination of the ship?
- What has happened in pirate movies you have seen?

Visualizing
- What does Long John Silver look like?

Monitoring Comprehension
- What does Long John tell Trelawney about his background?

Predicting
- What do you think will happen when the voyage begins?

Forming Questions
- What questions did you ask yourself when you were reading?
- Who has a question to ask the class about this passage?

Figure 4.2

Using Organizational Patterns

Sequence
- What things did Trelawney do in Bristol to prepare for the voyage?

Cause and Effect
- Why does Trelawney want a score of men (twenty) to man a ship that can be sailed with fewer sailors?

Compare and Contrast
- Compare Trelawney's opinion of Blandly to others' opinions.

Summarizing or Retelling

- Retell this segment of the story including as many details as you can.
- Retell this segment of the story including only the essential details.

Identifying Main Ideas

- How has Trelawney prepared for the expedition?
  (Main ideas often require inferences. That is the case with *Treasure Island,* for which a judgment needs to be tied in with the preparation.)

Inferring

- Do you trust Trelawney to be the leader of this expedition?
- What clues support his leadership abilities?
- What clues make you doubtful?

Using Fix-up Strategies

- When you read the list of enemies and did not understand any of those terms, what did you do?

Generalizing or Drawing Conclusions

- Was it dangerous sailing in the 1700s?
- Was the squire lucky to meet Long John Silver?
- What do we as readers know that Trelawney does not know?

Evaluating

- How much trust should you give a stranger?

Enjoying

- What adventures can you imagine will take place?

Text Features

(Many of the text features requiring attention have been addressed in the strategy list.)
1. Complicated sentence patterns: Trelawney keeps interrupting himself in the following sentence. What does the author do to help the reader? *The admirable fellow literally slaved in my interest, and so, I may say, did every one in Bristol, as soon as they got wind of the port we sailed for—treasure, I mean.*
2. In the story, there is unfamiliar vocabulary and perhaps some unfamiliar concepts. What are these things mentioned in the text that we have no familiarity with: schooner, public house, the immortal Hawke, fresh-water swabs?
(The teacher should provide answers for unknown concepts.)

Figure 4.2 (continued)

Chapter Four Summary

Guided reading is a time-consuming process, so it should be saved for getting the class into a book, for difficult passages, or for passages that offer an opportunity to practice a specific comprehension strategy. Once readers are off to a good start or safely over a difficult or important passage, they can read independently. Guided reading offers students a model, integrated directly into the literature they are reading, for the kind of questions they should be asking themselves as independent, expert readers.

TEACHER QUOTE

66 When I direct reading, I make an attempt to make a mental connection with the kids. I ask myself: What do they need to understand this lesson or story? Then I do a pre-reading activity that gets into their heads, and lets them know I am trying to create the best motivation I can to get them interested in the text. I always try to make a connection to their lives or to something they can identify with, and the lesson is guaranteed to be more successful. 99

—Mary Conrad, Reading Specialist
8th grade teacher
Aptakisic-Tripp C.C.S.D. 102
Buffalo Grove, IL

Chapter 4
Blackline Masters

◆ **Guided Reading Questions Planner for Promoting Reading Strategies**

◆ **Ideas for Classroom Use**

Choose a reading selection and use the planner to formulate questions to guide students in the reading process. It is not necessary to formulate questions for each topic listed in the planner. Choose topics that seem to best fit the text students are reading. Be sure to note any significant text features that may be new or difficult for students and spend time formulating questions or strategies to address these features. (Use Figure 4.2 as a guide and prompt as you formulate questions.)

Guided Reading Questions Planner
for Promoting Reading Strategies

Connecting Prior Background

_____

_____

_____

Recognizing Concepts

_____

_____

_____

Visualizing

Characters

_____

_____

Setting

_____

_____

Monitoring Comprehension

_____

_____

_____

Predicting

_____

_____

Forming Questions

What questions did you ask yourself when you were reading?

_____

_____

_____

Using Organizational Patterns

Sequence

_____

_____

Cause and Effect

_____

_____

Compare and Contrast

_____

_____

Topic/Subtopic

_____

_____

Problem/Solution

_____

_____

Summarizing or Retelling

Retell this segment of the story including as many details as you can.

_____

_____

_____

Retell this segment of the story including only the essential details.

_____

_____

_____

Identifying Main Ideas

_____

_____

_____

Using Fix-Up Strategies

Inferring

Generalizing or Drawing Conclusions

Evaluating

Enjoying

Text Features (Potential Obstacles)

Guided Reading Questions Planner (continued)

Looking at Questioning from Another Angle

Nothing has such power to broaden the mind as the ability to investigate systematically and truly all that comes under thy observation in life.

—MARCUS AURELIUS

Students need to respond to all types of questions. The recent Report of the National Reading Panel (Langenberg 2000) states that (1) answering questions and receiving immediate feedback and (2) generating questions are two of the seven categories of comprehension instruction that appeared to have a solid scientific basis for improving comprehension. (The other five are comprehension monitoring, cooperative learning, using graphic and semantic organizers, using story structure, and summarizing.) By thinking about, responding to, and generating a wide variety of questions, students learn to extend their definitions of reading beyond literal comprehension or simply copying answers. They also learn the types of questions readers need to ask themselves to monitor comprehension. Adult readers know that reading requires an intentional and thoughtful interaction between the reader and the text. Since not all students have yet reached this conclusion about reading, they need modeling, guidance, and practice.

Question-Answer Relationships (QAR)

In chapters 1 and 4, questioning was addressed as a way to help students develop reading strategies and make them aware of strategies for overcoming specific obstacles presented by the text. Those strategies were presented in a list, and lists are difficult to remember. A more organized and easier way to think about levels of comprehension and types of questions is the traditional method for defining levels of comprehension. Literal, literal rearranged, inferential, and critical are traditional levels of comprehension which work equally well for defining types of questions.

Adult readers know that reading requires an intentional and thoughtful interaction between the reader and the text. Since not all students have yet reached this conclusion about reading, they need modeling, guidance, and practice.

Taffy Raphael (1986) developed a completely parallel system to the traditional method that offers distinct advantages. Raphael was concerned that students frequently were asked questions in school but received no guidance on how to answer them. Every middle-grade teacher has had the experience of listening to a frustrated student say, "I spent hours looking for the answer, but it is not in the book," only to find out the question was, "What do you think . . .?" In response to her concern, Raphael developed a system called Question-Answer Relationships (QAR). Intended for fourth- through eighth-grade students, QAR teaches readers how to analyze the task demanded by the question in order to generate a strategy for answering it. Raphael named the types of questions so they would make more sense to students and so that the names would also describe the strategy used to find the answer. The question types are *right there, author and you, think and search,* and *on your own.*

Raphael's system has been substantiated by research. Raphael and Pearson (1982) found in their research that students in the fourth, sixth, and eighth grades who had been taught the strategy by a university researcher were more successful at answering questions than students who had not received the instruction. In a follow-up study (Tierney and Readence 2000), fourth-grade teachers who learned how to teach their students this strategy also received positive results.

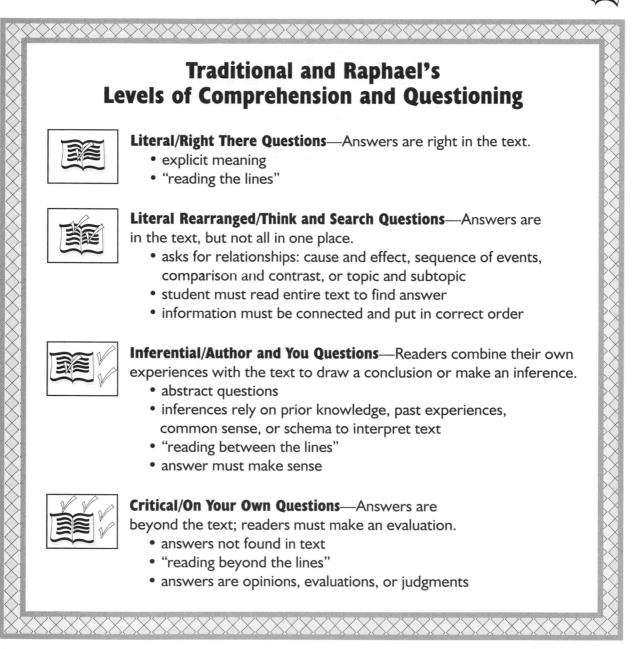

Traditional and Raphael's
Levels of Comprehension and Questioning

Literal/Right There Questions—Answers are right in the text.
- explicit meaning
- "reading the lines"

Literal Rearranged/Think and Search Questions—Answers are in the text, but not all in one place.
- asks for relationships: cause and effect, sequence of events, comparison and contrast, or topic and subtopic
- student must read entire text to find answer
- information must be connected and put in correct order

Inferential/Author and You Questions—Readers combine their own experiences with the text to draw a conclusion or make an inference.
- abstract questions
- inferences rely on prior knowledge, past experiences, common sense, or schema to interpret text
- "reading between the lines"
- answer must make sense

Critical/On Your Own Questions—Answers are beyond the text; readers must make an evaluation.
- answers not found in text
- "reading beyond the lines"
- answers are opinions, evaluations, or judgments

Figure 5.1

The two types of questioning systems—traditional and QAR—are not exclusive at all. Both Raphael's QAR and the traditional questioning taxonomies are discussed in detail in the following sections of this chapter. All of the types of questions that are used to develop strategies used by good readers or to decipher special requirements of the text fit relatively neatly into these four categories (see Figure 5.1).

Levels of Comprehension and Questioning

To be able to ask a broad range of questions, teachers must be thoroughly familiar with the different levels of comprehension and questioning. Readers at all grade levels need to answer all types of questions, although young readers may need extra guidance with inferential questions. To illustrate the application of questioning at all levels, I have chosen a primary text as an example, *The Tale of Peter Rabbit* (Potter 1955). It is even easier to devise these types of questions for upper-grade materials, where greater inference skills and critical reading skills are needed by the reader. See Figure 5.2 for sample questions; see the end of this chapter for a blackline planner.

Literal/Right There Questions

 Literal comprehension questions ask what the author said; that is, they ask for the explicit meaning. This type of questioning is sometimes called "reading the lines" because the answer exists in a single line of the text. It includes the who, what, when, and where. For *The Tale of Peter Rabbit,* the questions might be "Who were Peter's brothers and sisters?" and "Where did Mrs. Rabbit tell her children not to go?"

Raphael calls these types of questions *right there questions* because the answer is right there in the text. It could be underlined or copied, and often the same words that make up the answer are found in the question. Usually the single right answer comes directly from the text. Students typically need to understand what is literally happening before they can interpret the text, so teachers often start with some right there questions to make sure the basics of the story are clear. The easiest level of comprehension, right there questions are the easiest to answer.

During guided reading, the teacher not only asks content questions but also asks metacognitive strategy questions such as "How did you know that?" Students demonstrate how to find literal answers and how to substitute a synonym in the question to match the answer in the text. For example, most students can read the words *sand* and *bank*, but not all will understand what a *sand-bank* is. When students are exposed to this kind of modeling and supportive scaffolding, they begin to better understand the process as well as the content.

Sample Comprehension Question Planner
Questions for Each Type and Level of Comprehension

Comprehension Level	Description	Sample Questions
Literal/ Right There	The answers to these questions are at the easiest level of comprehension. Answers can be found right in the text in one location.	Where did Mrs. Rabbit tell her children not to go? Who are Peter's brothers and sisters?
Literal Rearranged/ Think and Search	The answers to these questions are explicitly stated but are not found all in one location. These questions ask for relationships such as cause and effect, sequence, comparison and contrast, or topic and subtopic.	What happened after Mr. McGregor first saw Peter? Where were all the places that Peter hid from Mr. McGregor?
Inferential/ Author and You	The answers to these questions are based on the text but also use past experience, common sense, or schema. They must be probable answers not just wild guesses.	Was Peter just naughty or curious? When the old mouse could not tell Peter where the gate was, why do you think Peter started to cry?
Critical/ On Your Own	The answers to these questions are not found in the text. They are questions of opinion, evaluation, or judgment.	What might happen if you go into someone's garden without permission? Should children be punished when they disobey their parents?

Figure 5.2

Literal Rearranged/
Think and Search Questions

The second tier to literal comprehension questions is literal rearranged questions. The entire answer to one of these questions is explicitly stated in the text but not all in one place. These types of questions show relationships such as cause and effect, sequence, comparison and contrast, or topic and subtopic. Of course, not every type of relationship is in every selection. Returning to *The Tale of Peter Rabbit,* the questions might be "What happened after Mr. McGregor first saw Peter?" and "Where were all the places that Peter hid from Mr. McGregor?"

Raphael calls these *think and search questions* because the answers have to be found in more than one place in the text. The student has to think about what is being asked, such as the cause, and then search for the effect. For example, Mrs. Rabbit told Peter not to go into Mr. McGregor's garden because Peter's father had an accident there and was put into a rabbit pie by Mrs. McGregor. Those two pieces of information are both given in the text but will not be found in the same location. Literal rearranged questions are more difficult than simple literal questions. The student whose strategy was to scan the text to find words that were similar to the question and copy down the sentence is now stymied, because that technique will no longer work. That reader soon realizes he must read the entire text to find both pieces of information that are necessary to solve the problem. When readers summarize or retell, they must connect all of the information into a correct sequence. Retelling requires that students are skilled at the literal rearranged level.

Inferential/Author and You Questions

Inferential questions require students to base their answers on the text but also to use past experiences, common sense, or schema to find reasonable answers to the questions. Inferences rely almost completely on prior knowledge (Pearson et al. 1999). Because the student must use both the text and personal experience, the inferential answer is not a wild guess. The answer must be probable, not just possible. Making inferences or interpretations is a higher and more difficult level of comprehension than simply recalling answers in the text because students must use two elements intertwined with each other. They must actively remember prior situations and connect them to the text. Students often need explicit instruction in making inferences because so many readers are used to simply looking for the answers in the text.

At the inferential level, the teacher might ask, "Was Peter naughty or just curious?" or "When the old mouse could not tell Peter where the gate was, why do you think Peter started to cry?" Raphael calls these types of questions *author and you questions,* because the answers are not solely in the text. Readers must interact with the text and draw upon their own experiences to interpret the information. Inferring, drawing conclusions, predicting, identifying the theme or moral, generalizing, and visualizing all require inferential skills.

Authors cannot tell the reader every little detail. They expect that the reader will be able to fill in missing information or read between the lines. Consider the line "While Jenny got ready for school, she thought about her big presentation." The author expects the reader to fill in that Jenny got out of bed, walked into the bathroom, took off her pajamas, turned on the shower, used the soap, rinsed off, got out of the shower, toweled dry, went to her dresser, found her clothes, got dressed, put on her shoes and socks, and so on. Some students approach reading in a straightforward manner and think their only task is to parrot what the text says, but they miss all the information between the lines.

Authors also expect readers to understand basic human emotional reactions and apply to the characters in the story what they have learned about how people act and react. In *The Sign of the Beaver* (Speare 1983), Matt will not use his new crutch until after the Indians have left his cabin. The author expects the reader to know Matt was embarrassed to try out something new and possibly difficult while strangers were watching him, so the author never directly says that Matt was embarrassed. Another inferential task is imagining how the story would be different if it were told from another character's point of view.

During guided reading, the teacher not only asks content questions but also asks metacognitive strategy questions such as "How did you know that?" When students are exposed to this kind of modeling and supportive scaffolding, they begin to better understand the process as well as the content.

Questions that require interpretation or inference are by definition more abstract than literal questions. Because inferential questions are abstract, many younger students may not be able to answer them independently without modeling by the teacher, although several studies provide evidence that students can improve their inferring skills as early as second grade (Pearson et al. 1999). Direct cueing can help. A cue for *The Tale of Peter Rabbit* might be: "How have you acted when you were really, really afraid?" Guided reading gives students scaffolding, cues, and clues about what information to use to draw an inference. It also gives them a chance to hear the processes used by other students for assembling information from two sources into one answer. Some readers, whatever their ages, do well with inferential questions because they always think and relate to their own experiences as they read, prefer the big picture, and cannot be bothered with small details, such as the answers to the picky literal questions.

Helping Students Become Inferential Readers

Activating prior knowledge or, in some cases, supplying background knowledge can help students become inferential readers. The teacher should choose concepts from the stories that are likely to be obstacles to comprehension. Concepts are more helpful than vocabulary. For example, a class was reading *The Cay* by Theodore Taylor (1969), in which a small blind boy and an old man were marooned on a Caribbean island surrounded by coral. To the students in this Midwestern class, coral was a lacy, delicate object sometimes found in fish tanks or jewelry and certainly nothing that could rip out the bottom of a boat. When the teacher supplied information about different types of sea coral, the class then understood why local fishing boats capable of rescuing the characters would not be sailing near the island.

Direct teaching of a concept, listening to other students who have experienced similar occurrences, and searching one's own memory all help bring that background knowledge to the foreground.

Direct teaching of a concept, listening to other students who have experienced similar occurrences, and searching one's own memory all help bring that background knowledge to the foreground. As the passage is read, both the text and the background can be woven together for deeper comprehension.

Critical/On Your Own Questions

Critical questions go beyond the text by asking questions of opinion, evaluation, or judgment. Critical comprehension can be thought of as reading beyond the lines. Raphael calls them *on your own questions* because the answers are not found in the book at all. These *questions* ask readers to think about and use their own experiences. The text material provides a jumping-off point and can contribute to the reader confirming, altering, or rejecting previous beliefs. Unlike inferential questions, even young students can answer on your own questions. As their parents can tell you, they are very opinionated from the earliest age, although they often lack the experiences that make for good judgment. Concerning *The Tale of Peter Rabbit,* the teacher could ask, "What might happen if you go into someone's garden without permission?" or "Should children be punished when they disobey their parents?" Critical questions can open up interesting and lively classroom discussions. They are often too complex, too abstract, or just too long for younger readers to write out the answers.

Students hone their reading and discussion skills if their teacher goes beyond questions such as "Who were Peter's brothers and sisters?" Teachers who give the class the opportunity to extend reading beyond the stated text with critical questions teach students that written text can provide the impetus for examining one's own beliefs.

Starting a Guided Reading Discussion

A good place to begin a guided reading discussion is with a critical/on your own question. For *The Tale of Peter Rabbit,* the teacher can ask, "What happened when you were some place you should not have been?" Encourage personal stories and guide the students toward some of the concepts they will encounter in the reading, such as feelings of fright, hiding to avoid being caught, disobeying a parent who had the child's safety in mind, and getting out of trouble. The readers become familiar with the topic or theme, many of the concepts, and much of the vocabulary. Everything will be fresh in the

Comprehension questions for *The Tale of Peter Rabbit:*

◆ What was the rabbit family going to do that day? (literal rearranged/think and search)

◆ Who were Peter's brother and sisters? (literal/right there)

◆ Where did Mrs. Rabbit tell her children not to go? (literal/right there)

◆ Why did Mrs. Rabbit tell her children not to go into Mr. McGregor's garden? (literal rearranged/think and search)

◆ Is Mrs. Rabbit bossy? (critical/on your own)

◆ What did Peter do? (literal rearranged/think and search)

◆ Was Peter naughty or just curious? (inferential/author and you)

◆ Why did Mr. McGregor want to chase nice little Peter out of his garden? (literal rearranged/think and search)

◆ What kind of problems might happen if you went into someone's garden without his permission? (critical/on your own)

minds of the students as they begin reading. This will aid comprehension as they will have schema, or a background, in which to incorporate the upcoming content.

Next, set a purpose and the length of the passage to be read. For example: "Read the first column on page 46 and find out what the rabbit family was going to do for the day." When the class has finished reading silently, it is time to ask questions. Ask questions in the order of the story, mixing all types of questions together.

Move on to the next section and have the students read the rest of the page and the following paragraph to find out what Peter did and then ask more questions.

Answers are usually oral, although some of the answers could be written down. As you walk around the room while the students are reading, glance at the written answers to assess comprehension of all of the students, not only those who had an opportunity to answer aloud. Several sections can be read in this manner. A short selection might be completed entirely with guided reading, or students might finish a longer selection independently once they are successfully on their way.

Closing Up the Discussion with Critical Questions

Once the students have examined the story of Peter Rabbit, do not stop there. The critical questions remind students that they should think about what they have read in a larger context than just the story. Critical questions can be the most intriguing questions to ask and answer. For example, "When Peter came home without his little blue jacket and both his shoes, what do you think Mrs. Rabbit said to him? What would your mother say to you?" and "Should children be punished when they disobey their parents?"

That last question could lead to quite a discussion. There will be all kinds of provisos and opinions. Be sure to bring Peter and his experience back into the discussion because there is a good lesson to be learned. Students do not automatically transfer the lesson from the story to their own lives unless the teacher provides a specific bridge. David Perkins and Gabriel Salomon (1992) state that teachers can help students transfer information learned in one context—the story—to a more generalized setting—their lives—by asking students how what they learned from one topic might apply elsewhere. Guiding students to explore in detail the similarities and differences between two situations also facilitates transfer. The students who kick each other as they leave the classroom after reading a story about respect and human kindness do not have a teacher who encouraged transfer.

The Guided Reading Planner blackline at the end of this chapter will help teachers ensure that they ask questions at all levels of comprehension. The planner also includes three additional questions teachers need to ask themselves in order to compose the questions:

◆ What difficult features does the text present?

◆ What are my students' abilities and background knowledge?

◆ What special strategies or goals do I need to teach according to my curriculum?

When teachers have considered the answers to these three questions, they will compose questions that will be a perfect match to the students, the text, and the curriculum.

Teachers must be sure to ask how students found the answers, what information they used to reach their conclusions, what they knew that was similar, and how they knew what unfamiliar things such as a *sand-bank* were. Reflecting on and naming the comprehension strategies makes guided reading powerful. Otherwise, it is just a question-and-answer period led by the teacher. Remember that the final objective is to develop independent readers who pose questions to themselves while reading.

Turning Questioning Skills into Questioning Strategies

When students understand how the reading process works, they have learned a skill. When they can use that skill on their own, it becomes a strategy. With questioning, the object is to help readers develop their own questions while reading independently. As adult readers, we seldom realize we do this except when something has not made immediate sense. Then we question ourselves—"I wonder why Dr. Scarpetta said that to Marino?"—thinking that something is out of character. At that point, we often go back and reread. We must find out the word was *uselessness* instead of *usefulness,* which of course changes the whole meaning. As adults, we sometimes stop hours or days later and consider how something we read applies to the situation we are now in. When we think of self-questioning, it does not mean that students stop in the middle of a text to ask themselves sets of questions any more than we do as adults. We ask questions as a part of monitoring comprehension, especially when it does not make sense.

One way to help students build the strategy of self-questioning is to ask them to develop questions about what they are reading instead of just answering questions. The QAR strategy lends itself to this purpose very well. As students are reading text, the teacher can ask questions and identify the question type. The teacher can then ask students to read the next section and develop the same type of questions. Students think this is fun and are easily able to develop the questions following teacher modeling.

The QAR strategy also transfers very well when a student is stuck on a question. The teacher can cue the student by saying, "This is a think and search question. You can find the answer in the text, but it is not all in one place." Since the student now knows what he has to do to find the answer, he will think and search and most likely locate the other part of the answer.

Chapter Five Summary

Classroom discussion is at the heart of reading instruction, especially when it is really a discussion and not just a literal question-and-answer session. By including questions at all levels of comprehension and having students develop questions as well as answers, you can improve classroom interaction and classroom climate as well as reading skills.

TEACHER QUOTE

❝ I feel like directed reading puts my voice in their heads. I guide their reading and teach them the strategies to use while reading. It's like my voice is right there modeling what they should be looking for or what strategies to use to solve a reading problem they may encounter. I am their internal voice.

My enthusiasm to the reading process and my love of the material often is the impetus to make then want to read. When I tell them a story is great, I mean it. I get excited just talking about what they are going to read. My joy of reading is contagious. ❞

—Mary Conrad, Reading Specialist
8th grade teacher
Aptakisic-Tripp C.C.S.D. 102
Buffalo Grove, IL

Chapter 5 Blackline Masters

◆ Question Planners
- Comprehension Question Planner
- Guided Reading Planner

◆ Comprehension Questions Planner
- Choose a simple story (or short text sample or other short piece) and write out sample questions using the Comprehension Question Planner. Use this story and planner to teach students the four levels of questions, before moving on to more complicated stories and more extensive questions.
- Choose a simple story (or short text sample or other short piece) and give a copy of the Comprehension Question Planner to each student. Ask students to write sample questions for the story using the Sample Question Planner.
- Choose a story or text with several sections and use the Guided Reading Planner to devise a plan for leading a guided reading session. Be sure to consider any difficult text features, students' abilities and backgrounds, and specific strategies or goals before you devise questions at each level. Also remember to choose a purpose-setting question for each section that will grab students' attention and facilitate better comprehension as they read the text.

Comprehension Question Planner
Questions for Each Type and Level of Comprehension

Comprehension Level	Description	Sample Questions
Literal/ Right There	The answers to these questions are at the easiest level of comprehension. Answers can be found right in the text in one location.	
Literal Rearranged/ Think and Search	The answers to these questions are explicitly stated but are not found all in one location. These questions ask for relationships such as cause and effect, sequence, comparison and contrast, or topic and subtopic.	
Inferential/ Author and You	The answers to these questions are based on the text but also use past experience, common sense, or schema. They must be probable answers not just wild guesses.	
Critical/ On Your Own	The answers to these questions are not found in the text. They are questions of opinion, evaluation, or judgment.	

Guided Reading Planner

Difficult text features:

_____

_____

Students' abilities and background knowledge:

_____

_____

Special strategies or goals to teach:

_____

_____

First section p. ___ to ___

Purpose-setting question:

_____

Right there question:

_____

Prove it. How did you know?

Think and search question:

_____

Where did you find the two parts? How do they fit together?

Author and you question:

_____

How did you know that? Why is that a likely answer?

On your own question:

_____

Why do you think so?

Second section p. ___ to ___

Purpose-setting question:

_____

Right there question:

_____

Prove it. How did you know?

Think and search question:

_____

Where did you find the two parts? How do they fit together?

Author and you question:

_____

How did you know that? Why is that a likely answer?

On your own question:

_____

Why do you think so?

Next section p. ___ to ___

Purpose-setting question:

_____

Right there question:

_____

Prove it. How did you know?

Think and search question:

_____

Where did you find the two parts? How do they fit together?

Guided Reading Planner (continued)

Author and you question:

_____

How did you know that? Why is that a likely answer?

On your own question:

_____

Why do you think so?

Next section p. ___ to ___

Purpose-setting question:

_____

Right there question:

_____

Prove it. How did you know?

Think and search question:

_____

Where did you find the two parts? How do they fit together?

Author and you question:

_____

How did you know that? Why is that a likely answer?

On your own question:

_____

Why do you think so?

Last section p. ___ to ___

Purpose-setting question:

_____

Right there question:

_____

Prove it. How did you know?

Think and search question:

_____

Where did you find the two parts? How do they fit together?

Author and you question:

_____

How did you know that? Why is that a likely answer?

On your own question:

_____

Why do you think so?

Planning Notes:

_____

_____

_____

_____

_____

_____

_____

_____

_____

_____

_____

_____

Guided Reading Planner (continued)

Variations on Guided Reading

Variety's the very spice of life,
That gives it all its flavour.

—WILLIAM COWPER

There are many variations on the theme of guided reading. The version a teacher chooses can depend on the features of the text, the needs of the students, or a curriculum feature or reading strategy that the teacher wants to emphasize. A text with a strong plot may lend itself to more extensive prediction. Using the overhead with guided reading and a process called Directed Reading Thinking Activity are good choices for focusing on prediction. Any text may call for visualization. Other techniques such as think-alouds or reciprocal reading that may not actually fall under the umbrella of guided reading can still accomplish the same goals. As students become more independent readers or when the teacher cannot read with students, the teacher can become a virtual guided reading teacher by providing embedded questions or stop-and-go questions. All of these variations are discussed in this chapter.

Directed Reading Thinking Activity (DRTA)

Predicting is a very powerful motivational and thinking tool. It is also relatively risk free, so it encourages high participation. Students love to predict and then read to find out if they were right. They typically approach story predictions as puzzles, trying out different solutions and hoping their favorite prediction will be the one chosen by the author. Teachers should promote discussion of the varied predictions to build anticipation for the story (Richek 1987). Prediction not only builds excitement, it also teaches students to set their own purposes for reading and not to passively accept whatever is before their eyes, whether it seems sensible or not.

Predicting requires that students think logically and inferentially about the direction of the story and then use their own experiences in conjunction with the text to hypothesize. They can call upon their memories of similar stories, personal experiences, and movie plots to justify their predictions. This bank of organized prior experiences is called schema or schemata. Once students understand that a "right" prediction is not needed and any reasonable, justifiable answer will be accepted, they will volunteer guesses and support or challenge other predictions with enthusiasm.

When prediction becomes a central feature of guided reading, the process becomes Directed Reading Thinking Activity (DRTA). Originally developed by Russell Stauffer in 1969, DRTA has never gone out of style. The first step in DRTA is asking the students to speculate what the story or passage might be about. After the students give several possible answers, they read the text to support or refute their predictions (Nessel 1989). In DRTA, after the students finish reading the passage, the teacher asks if their predictions were justified or if they have changed their minds. The teacher should be sure to ask what caused them to change their predictions and to make new ones. See Figure 6.1 for DRTA steps.

For *Charlotte's Web* (White 1952), the teacher can ask, "How do you think Charlotte is going to save Wilbur?" Some will predict an escape through the fence, some might imagine a barnyard revolt, some will predict intervention from Fern, and some might guess that Charlotte has a plan up her sleeve. Encourage several predictions and have the students explain what brought them to those conclusions. Then let the students read to find out what does happen to Wilbur. The enthusiasm of the students will be surprising.

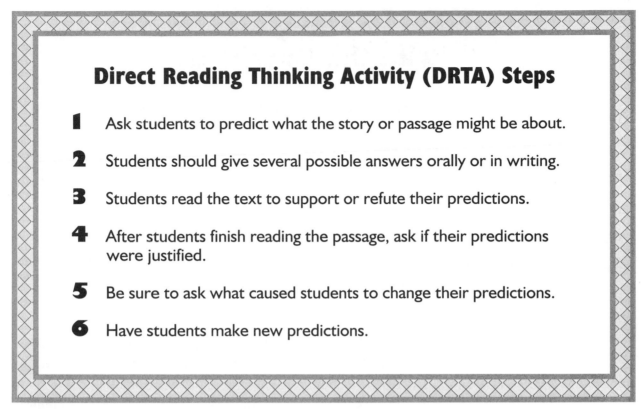

Direct Reading Thinking Activity (DRTA) Steps

1 Ask students to predict what the story or passage might be about.

2 Students should give several possible answers orally or in writing.

3 Students read the text to support or refute their predictions.

4 After students finish reading the passage, ask if their predictions were justified.

5 Be sure to ask what caused students to change their predictions.

6 Have students make new predictions.

Figure 6.1

Multiple literal questions are usually not necessary with DRTA because students must justify their opinions by recalling important points anyway (Nessel 1989). After finishing a DRTA lesson, the teacher can go back to the story to use it again to teach or refine other skills or strategies. This second reading may be a better time for noticing multiple meanings of words, common suffixes, or text features. Doing all this on the first reading would interrupt the flow of the story and thus disrupt comprehension. The DRTA method of extending and refining skills was originally recommended by Stauffer to encourage accuracy in reading in addition to speculation, but the second step sometimes falls by the wayside.

DRTA is a natural fit with guided reading. As readers use information in the story and information from their own backgrounds to make predictions, the teacher can guide the discussion and show how to integrate the two kinds of knowledge into the dynamic process of constructing meaning. Teachers can also help students decide which pieces of information are more important in the process. Being able to decide what is important and not attending to insignificant details are characteristics of good readers.

Guided Reading and Predicting with the Overhead

Being able to decide what is important and not attending to insignificant details are characteristics of good readers.

Another variation of predicting with guided reading can be done with the whole class. The teacher can type a story and photocopy it onto a transparency for the overhead projector. It is important to choose a short story that is unpredictable or could have several possible twists. The teacher may place a very short story or just the beginning of a longer story on the transparency. Next, the story should be divided into sections, sometimes stopping in the middle of a sentence: "And then he saw a . . ." The teacher should be sure to use large enough type so the students can easily see the story.

Covering the unread sections, the teacher invites the class to read along one section at a time, asking for predictions and justifications, visualizations, and inferences. The teacher should remember to ask at what point students changed their minds and what information they used to change their predictions. For students who are timid about guessing, the teacher might ask, "Do you think that Julie is right, or do you agree with Mike?" It is important that everyone is involved. Every student can participate in the predicting because no one can read ahead; everyone has an equal chance of being right or wrong. Students can listen to the reasoning of classmates, venture a guess, and then eagerly read the author's actual ending.

Visualization

Another strategy that can be used with guided reading is visualization. Good readers develop pictures in their heads about what the characters look like, the places the characters are, what they are doing, and whether a character walks with mincing steps or long strides. They start to build pictures in their minds and adjust the size of the room, the lankiness of the hero, and the gender of a character named Pat as additional information is given by the author. The best readers will say they do not simply develop pictures; they create an entire movie.

When students recall information, some of it is attached to the pictures they have visualized for themselves. There is a dramatic scene in *Roll of Thunder, Hear My Cry* by Mildred Taylor (1977) in which the father, Mr. Logan, is run over by his own wagon while trying to change a wheel during a storm. When a group of students in one of my classes was asked about what happened, a big debate ensued over where the father was standing and if the wagon rolled forward or backward when the horse reared up. The imagery attached to that scene enhanced the readers' memories until they were absolutely positive that the author had written the scene exactly as they saw it. Developing mental images provides two particular advantages (Tierney and Readence 2000): Readers develop a framework for organizing and remembering information, and, as students develop images they expend more energy for integrating information. Both comprehension and recall increase.

Teachers should model generating mental imagery (Tierney and Readence 2000). Teachers can do this by reading a passage with the students, followed by an oral description of what the teacher imagined. Teachers should include many of the same details that appear in the passage, retold in their own words, as well how they saw the action. Using the *Treasure Island* passage found earlier in this book, a teacher might say:

> "I see old Long John Silver walking around the wharf, trying to look casual but keeping an eye out for Squire Trelawney. Then I see him just standing at the end of the pier, close but not too near to where the squire will be, pretending to smell the salt air. He is a big burley man and wears a bright blue short jacket. When the squire says good morning, Long John works hard to keep a conversation going, but he tries to look disinterested, waiting for a break to tell his so-called life story. He puffs on a pipe and tries not to look too interested as he describes his talents as an honorable sailor and a fine cook, just waiting for the squire to take the bait."

Teachers should conclude with a comment similar to: "The images I make in my mind will help me understand what I have read" (Tierney and Readence 2000).

Students then share their mental images of the next passage. The similarities and differences of the images students shared will help students clarify and refine their use of imagery. For independent practice, teachers can recommend the use of visualization with additional texts that lend themselves to mental imagery. For situations that do not lend themselves as readily to visualization, teachers can direct or guide students to use additional strategies such as predicting or self-questioning to complement imaging (Tierney and Readence 2000).

> **The best readers will say they do not simply develop pictures; they create an entire movie.**

Teachers can encourage mental imaging during guided reading by asking questions. Using *Harry Potter and the Sorcerer's Stone* (Rowling 1997), teachers can ask: "What did the interior of the train carriage on the Hogwarts Express look like?" Some students will be totally startled and others' first response will be that the text did not say. However, as the students begin to each build an image in their minds' eyes, they redraw the entire event, as well as the appearance of the train. The facts, the sequence, and the image are all strengthened. During guided reading, asking students what they used to construct the image will draw them back to clues in the text and encourage them to integrate their own knowledge of the world with the story.

After guided reading, teachers can also ask students to draw their own illustrations for the story. Middle- and upper-grade students can sequence the selection with a series of pictures or they can go back to a section of text and take notes for an illustrator. They must decide which aspects cannot be changed because they are specifically described in the text and which aspects they would like to fill in through visualization. The students acquire skills in visualizing and the drawings also serve as a very good assessment of their comprehension.

Primary students can listen to a story without being shown the pictures in the book. The following is an excellent idea for a primary class (Graves et al. 1998). The teacher reads a story aloud as the students close their eyes and listen. During the first few pages, the teacher models the strategy and shares his or her own mental pictures. As the teacher reads the remainder of the story, he or she reminds students to visualize what they are hearing. The teacher can ask:

◆ What is the main character doing?

◆ Who is he seeing here?

◆ Can you picture it in your mind?

The teacher asks the students to describe what they imagined and tells them they will get to draw a picture from the story. After reading the story again, the teacher discusses what happened in the beginning, the middle, and the end. Students are asked to count off by threes and to put their numbers on the backs of their papers. Those with number one will each draw a picture from the beginning; the twos will draw a picture from the middle; and the threes will draw a picture from the end. The next day, the teacher selects a set of three pictures and in mixed order has the students who drew them tell about the scenes. Then have the class sequence them correctly. The process can be repeated with several sets of pictures, providing practice in visualizing, retelling, and sequencing.

Think-Alouds

Although think-alouds are not normally thought of as guided reading, they accomplish many of the same purposes as guided reading does, especially monitoring comprehension and self-questioning. To model a think-aloud, the teacher reads a passage and intersperses thinking aloud with reading, thus demonstrating the processing of an expert reader in order to identify the specific strategies being used (Kucan and Beck 1997).

The teacher may wonder aloud what will happen next and then make a prediction. As the teacher reads further along in the passage, she can identify when the prediction is confirmed or rejected and predict again. The teacher can describe a visual image of the text. When something is misread or a thought is lost, the teacher thinks aloud to choose a strategy to fix up the comprehension loss. The teacher might say, "Well, this does not seem to fit in. I had better think about what was happening or read that sentence again." Students see and hear strategies for self-monitoring and learn that even expert readers may have to redirect, reread, or reconsider. Of course, what teachers choose to think aloud depends on the needs of the students, the special difficulties of the text, or the reading goals that they have in mind for their students.

> **T**he five most important strategies for modeling think-alouds are:
>
> ◆ Forming good hypotheses (Predicting)
>
> ◆ Making mental images (Visualizing)
>
> ◆ Making analogies or showing how prior knowledge applies
>
> ◆ Monitoring comprehension
>
> ◆ Demonstrating fix-up strategies
>
> Adpated from Davey (1983).

During guided reading, the teacher may stop and ask a student to think aloud about the last paragraph or passage. It can be difficult to get students to tell about the process instead of just summarizing the passage; good readers process almost unconsciously. Sufficient teacher modeling helps. To build a bridge from demonstration to independent use after teacher modeling, ask students to read in pairs and think aloud to each other, and then have them read independently and think to themselves. Practice partner think-alouds in the classroom by using a "say something" technique. At the end of every page, students must turn to their partners and say something. Without teacher modeling, they usually just retell events on the page, which can be useful for monitoring comprehension. With teacher modeling, the students are more likely to evaluate the content, think of a similarity, discuss the process, or tell which part was difficult to understand. Older students can write something instead.

As a final step for self-monitoring of independent reading, teachers can make a chart with the five strategies listed on the left side. Across the top of the chart are designations for degrees of use for the strategies. After reading a selection, students must evaluate their own strategies and put checks in the boxes that describe their independent reading. A think-aloud chart is especially effective for difficult passages. (See Figure 6.2.)

Reciprocal Reading

Reciprocal reading, developed by Annemarie Palincsar and Ann Brown (1984), shares many of the techniques of guided reading, including scaffolded instruction and gradual release of responsibility to students. Reciprocal reading is used with expository text, although it works quite well with narrative text also. It is a specific procedure that takes some time for students to learn and internalize; twenty practice sessions are recommended to achieve the desired results (Graves et al. 1998).

Students first read a short passage. How short the passage is depends on the grade level. The stopping point is determined by how ideas or events are grouped. Using short passages is especially helpful because they are brief enough so they do not overwhelm the struggling reader.

Sample Self-Monitoring Think-Aloud Strategies Chart

Name: Sue

	not at all	much of the time	all of the time
I *predicted* what would happen next.		✔	
I *visualized* the characters and scenes.			✔
I *connected* what I read to other events.		✔	
I *identified problems in comprehension.*	✔		
I used *fix-up strategies* when I didn't understand what I read at first.		✔	

CHART ADAPTED FROM DAVEY, BETH. (1983, OCTOBER) "THINK ALOUD: MODELING THE COGNITIVE PROCESSES OF READING COMPREHENSION" PG. 46. *JOURNAL OF READING,* 27(1), 44–47. REPRINTED WITH PERMISSION OF THE INTERNATIONAL READING ASSOCIATION. ALL RIGHTS RESERVED.

Figure 6.2

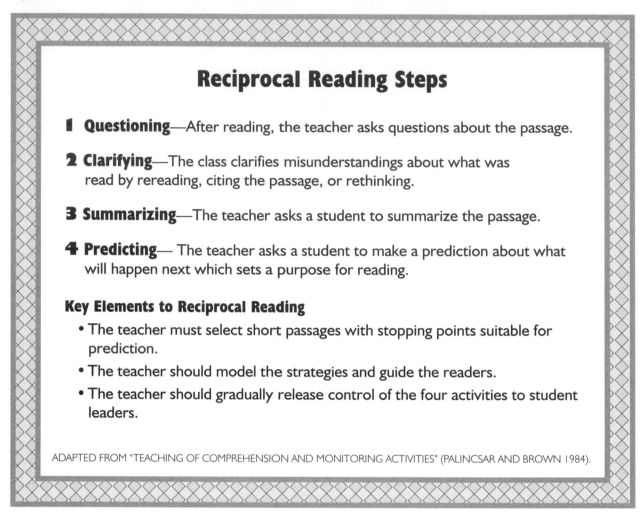

> # Reciprocal Reading Steps
>
> **1 Questioning**—After reading, the teacher asks questions about the passage.
>
> **2 Clarifying**—The class clarifies misunderstandings about what was read by rereading, citing the passage, or rethinking.
>
> **3 Summarizing**—The teacher asks a student to summarize the passage.
>
> **4 Predicting**— The teacher asks a student to make a prediction about what will happen next which sets a purpose for reading.
>
> **Key Elements to Reciprocal Reading**
> - The teacher must select short passages with stopping points suitable for prediction.
> - The teacher should model the strategies and guide the readers.
> - The teacher should gradually release control of the four activities to student leaders.
>
> ADAPTED FROM "TEACHING OF COMPREHENSION AND MONITORING ACTIVITIES" (PALINCSAR AND BROWN 1984).

Figure 6.3

Reciprocal reading has four steps: questioning, clarifying, summarizing, and predicting. After everyone has finished reading the passage, the teacher or a student leader asks questions about the passage. If there are any problems or misunderstandings, the class clarifies the issues by rereading, citing the passage, or rethinking. Someone then summarizes the passage and makes a prediction about the next section. At first, teachers model the strategies and guide the readers, gradually releasing control of the four activities to student leaders. See Figure 6.3 for Reciprocal Reading Steps.

Questioning

The teacher first models questioning by asking various questions and drawing the students' attention to the types of questions that were asked. The teacher may use the traditional question categories—literal, literal rearranged, inferential, and critical—or QAR question categories—right there, think and search, author and you, and on your own. Teachers of older students ask them to develop questions according to the same criteria. Learning to ask good questions takes a great deal of practice and modeling, because students tend to stick to the trivia questions. If teachers write the categories on the board and identify each question they ask, students will imitate their models. Teachers can guide question development by prompting, "The reader first needs to know a simple fact about what happened when the foghorn stopped." A student might respond, "What does the monster do after the foghorn is turned off?"

Younger students do not have to know as much as the teacher does about the underlying levels of comprehension. Younger students can usually do quite well by just defining the types of questions as skinny questions and fat questions. For older students, it may help to define questions as fact questions and discussion questions. Learning the difference takes some time, but a simple definition could be that skinny questions ask who, what, when, and where while fat questions ask why or how. Another simple definition is that fact questions can be answered in one sentence with only one reasonable answer while discussion questions require more than one sentence with several reasonable answers.

> For younger students, define the types of questions as follows:
>
> ◆ **Skinny questions** ask who, what, when, and where.
>
> ◆ **Fat questions** ask why or how.
>
> For older students, define the types of questions as follows:
>
> ◆ **Fact questions** can be answered in one sentence with only one reasonable answer.
>
> ◆ **Discussion questions** require answers with more than one sentence with several reasonable answers.

Clarifying

During the second step of reciprocal reading, clarifying, unexpected answers may cause everyone to go back to the text to clarify the issues and see if there was a misinterpretation or if the answer was an inference that no one else had considered. Questions that are particularly useful for clarifying problem areas are: "What did you find difficult to understand?" and "What might an average fourth-grader find difficult to understand?" Students must give responses to those questions; they cannot cover up by answering that everything was perfectly clear. Those two general questions seem to help on two levels. Anything that was uncertain—perhaps an interpretation, perhaps a critical vocabulary word, perhaps a missed connection—is cleared up on the spot. The other benefit is the realization that all readers find certain passages difficult, and even the best readers go back or stop to reconsider. Students can also ask clarification questions at this point in reciprocal reading. The clarification stage, however, is the most difficult for students to complete on their own (Pearson et al. 1999).

Summarizing

The next step in reciprocal reading, summarizing, is always challenging. The ability to figure out what was crucial and what was irrelevant is a distinguishing mark of good readers. Students and the teacher can critique the chosen main points as the class discusses what was essential and what was not. The whole passage becomes clearer as the minor details are swept away and the main points are firmed up. Hearing the summary can be very helpful to other students because, when the story is clarified, they feel secure once again and are motivated to move on to the next part.

Predicting

In predicting, the last step of reciprocal reading, students set a purpose for reading the next section. Students predict the event or topic of the next section as they draw on previous story knowledge, their own personal knowledge, organization of expositional texts, or knowledge of plot lines. If students' predictions are confirmed, their ideas about text organization are confirmed. If their predictions are not confirmed, they learn to align their thoughts more closely to common organizational patterns.

With teacher modeling, the students are more likely to evaluate the content, think of a similarity, discuss the process, or tell which part was difficult to understand.

Once the teacher and students learn the pattern, the reciprocal reading method proceeds faster than it would seem, though it still is a time-consuming process. However, the time invested is worth it when students are perfectly clear about what they read and have experienced the processes that good readers use.

As the teacher releases responsibility to the students, cooperative group work can follow as students become familiar with the procedure. Students can ask one another questions, then clarify, summarize, and predict as a group. Rotating roles in groups of four works very well. The tasks can also rotate with an uneven number of students, but having some kind of tangible marker to designate who currently has each role helps avoid confusion. In smaller groups, everyone gets to have a turn more often, so students attain greater proficiency at developing the skills, and participation is more active. Janice Almasi (1995) found that peer-led discussions are very powerful. In her award-winning doctoral dissertation of 1994, Almasi reported that there was richer and more complex interaction among peers than there was during teacher-led discussions. Also, there was greater retention of the thinking processes in which the students engaged. As students repeat the process, they can progress from working in groups to reading independently. This takes time for the various levels of practice, but the gradual release of responsibility leads to making self-questioning, self-clarifying, summarizing, and predicting a habit.

> **V**ariations on Guided Reading:
>
> ◆ Directed Reading Thinking Activity (DRTA)
> ◆ Predicting
> ◆ Visualization
> ◆ Think-Alouds
> ◆ Reciprocal Reading
> ◆ Student-Created Questions
> ◆ Virtual Guided Reading

Student-Created Questions

For variety, there are two interesting and simplified permutations: having students write questions and having students question the teacher. For a written assignment in responding to reading, the teacher may ask the readers to write questions instead of answers. The questions by themselves will give the teacher a good indication of comprehension. A team challenge might follow. The other alternative for teachers willing to put themselves in the learner's role is to ask students to develop questions that the teacher has to answer. If teachers prove their answers by rereading the relevant parts of the text or by explaining their reasoning process, they demonstrate another way to model what good readers do.

All readers find certain passages difficult, and even the best readers go back or stop to reconsider what they have read.

Stop-and-Go Questions

Stop-and-go questions are for students who are reading more independently. The questions follow the same order as the story and set a purpose for reading while keeping the students engaged. Students read the first question and then read the selection until they come to the answer. They then stop to write down the answer to the question. Students follow the same procedure for question two, continuing with the process until they have answered all of the questions. Stop-and-go questions, like embedded questions, can also be used for a select number of students, providing another low-profile intervention. If the teacher uses the questions for the whole class, the better readers will probably read the entire selection and then return to answer the questions. They are already monitoring their comprehension and do not want to have the story interrupted. The students who still need guidance in identifying the most important points in the story like the stop-and-go procedure. They find it easier to read with a purpose set by the teacher, and the questions keep them on track.

A sample of stop-and-go questions also uses *Treasure Island,* and provides questions at the literal, literal rearranged, and inferential levels, although the question about Captain Flint's character may also be a critical question (Figure 6.5). This is also a great passage for developing mental images. In a real assignment, the questions probably would not be clustered so closely together, but the sample is sufficient to give an idea of how the technique works.

KidsClick!

If you like reading *Treasure Island* and are considering it for the classroom, there is a fabulous Web site that links to all kinds of interesting support material for several books.

The site is called *KidsClick! Literature* and can be found at **<http://sunsite.berkeley.edu/KidsClick!/toplite.html>**.

Select "Books, Classic" then click on "Treasure Island." The Treasure Island site can be directly accessed at **<http://www.ukoln.ac.uk/services/treasure>**.

The site contains a wide array of very useful background material, including:

◆ biographical information on the author, Robert Louis Stevenson;

◆ links to other sites about the author;

◆ a summary of the entire book;

◆ sketches of the characters;

◆ links to information on ships, pirates, treasures, tropical islands; and

◆ other related subjects.

Students can also send in book reviews, find other fiction and nonfiction library books about pirates, design a pirate, and take a quiz. Teachers can find the outline of an entire unit teaching plan and a parent letter. (The entire online text is also available, but unfortunately takes too long to download.)

Sample of Stop-and-Go Questions for *Treasure Island*

1. **Even with the map, why will it be hard to locate the treasure?**

2. **Why was the sailor shrieking?**

3. **What was odd about the body?**

4. **How do you suppose the body came to be there? What was its purpose?**

5. **What did you learn about the character of Captain Flint?**

As we pulled over, there was some discussion on the chart. The red cross was, of course, far too large to be a guide. "Tall tree, Spy-glass shoulder, bearing a point to the N. of N. N. E., Skeleton Island E. S. E. and by E. Ten feet." Every here and there, one of a different species rose forty or fifty feet clear of its neighbours, and which of these was the particular "tall tree" of Captain Flint could only be decided on the spot, and by the readings of the compass.

Bending to our left, we began to ascend the slope toward the plateau. We had proceeded for about half a mile, and were approaching the brow of the plateau, when the man upon the farthest left began to cry aloud as if in terror. Shout after shout came from him, and the others began to run in his direction.

At the foot of a pretty big pine, a human skeleton lay, with a few shreds of clothing, on the ground. I believe a chill struck for a moment to every heart.

"He was a seaman," said George Merry, who bolder than the rest, had gone up close, and was examining the rags of clothing. "Leastways, this is good sea-cloth. But what sort of a way is that for bones to lie? 'Tain't in natur'."

Indeed, on a second glance, it seemed impossible to fancy that the body was in a natural position. But for some disarray the man lay perfectly straight—his feet pointing in one direction, his hands, raised above his head like a diver's pointing directly in the opposite.

"I've taken a notion into my old numskull," observed Silver. "Here's the compass; there's the tip-top p'int o' Skeleton Island, stickin' out like a tooth. Just take a bearing, will you, along the line of them bones." The body pointed straight in the direction of the island, and the compass read duly E. S. E. and by E. "I thought so. This here is a p'inter. Flint hauled him here and laid him down to be the compass, shiver my timbers!"

STORY EXCERPTED FROM *TREASURE ISLAND* (STEVENSON 1939).

Figure 6.5

Chapter Six Summary

Guided reading and all its variations provide support for the reader while reading text silently. It provides a model of what an expert reader actually does while reading. Through examining content and reading strategies simultaneously, the reader becomes more consciously aware of the reading process. These techniques are especially useful for beginning a reading selection or for difficult passages. Students who have difficulty maintaining focus, whose first language is not English, or who are inexperienced in making comprehension their primary goal benefit the most from the use of these techniques. The strategies supplied through guided reading provide the bridge to becoming an expert, independent reader.

TEACHER QUOTE

" As a child I had Think and Do workbooks. Very little thinking was involved, and the only doing was choosing answers. It was very tidy. The teacher would pile up the workbooks, check the work, and give them back to us. It didn't expand our thinking.

Writing replaces workbooks now. Because of the nature of writing and thinking, writing can't be copied from someone else. Each person has a unique way of explaining their ideas, representing their thoughts, expressing their feelings, and it is not possible to copy someone else's thoughts.

We can talk without thinking; I often do. But we can't write without thinking. So give the children a pen, some paper, time and a quite room, and let the thinking begin. "

—Pat Braun, Reading Specialist
6th grade teacher
Roosevelt School, River Forest, IL

Chapter 6
Blackline Masters

◆ Blackline Master for Guided Reading Variations

- Self-Monitoring Think-Aloud Strategies Chart

◆ Ideas for Classroom Use

- Choose a passage to read. Show an overhead transparency of the Think-Aloud Strategies chart as you read the passage and model the think-aloud strategy. Point out the strategies you use as you use them. When you are finished reading the passage, go back and evaluate how well you used each strategy. Ask students to help you evaluate your demonstration.

- Give a copy of the chart to student partners. Ask partners to read a passage together, stopping at the end of each page to turn to their partners and think aloud together. Ask students to be aware of the think-aloud strategies listed on the chart and to avoid retelling the passages to their partners. When partners have finished reading the entire passage, ask them to evaluate their use of think-aloud strategies using the chart.

- Give a copy of the chart to each student. Explain each strategy and encourage students to monitor themselves as they read a short passage. Assign students a short passage to read independently. When students are finished reading, ask them to fill out the chart to evaluate their use of the think-aloud strategies.

Self-Monitoring Think-Aloud Strategies Chart

Name: _____

	not at all	much of the time	all of the time
I *predicted* what would happen next.			
I *visualized* the characters and scenes.			
I *connected* what I read to other events.			
I *identified problems in comprehension*.			
I used *fix-up strategies* when I didn't understand what I read at first.			

Guided Reading with Content Textbooks

*Knowledge is of two kinds. We know a
subject ourselves, or we know where we can
find information upon it.*

—Samuel Johnson

"If you look in the middle school and high school classrooms to examine the role of expository text, you are virtually forced to conclude that it has none." This extraordinary statement was made by P. David Pearson, a reading researcher and the former dean of the College of Education at the University of Illinois (Beck et al. 1999, 371). He made this statement because so many students do not bother to read the textbook assignments they are given. Teachers, knowing that their students get so little from textbooks even when they do read them, often cover the same material orally in class the next day. Some teachers have almost given up using their texts because the material seems beyond the abilities of their students. While these reactions are some-what understandable, they certainly are counterproductive—someday, as college students, workers, or adults fulfilling daily requirements, their students will have to read and understand expository text.

Textbooks and Expository Texts

There are several reasons students often get very little out of reading text-book assignments. Textbooks are significantly different from narrative stories. First, the text is almost always a topic/subtopic expositional format. Both the vocabulary loads and concept loads are dense. Textbooks have different text features than novels, adding purpose-setting questions, boldface topics and subtopics that offer organizational clues, review questions, and summary statements to the already tightly packed format. Textbooks also offer a variety of graphics—maps, charts, photos, illustrations, diagrams, and captions under pictures—which can be invaluable for condensing information and illustrating examples and relationships. No section can be skipped over. The usual response of students, however, is to do just that. Students routinely skip all of these features, because they do not consider them an actual part of the reading assignment.

In addition, the language in texts can be very difficult. Texts are often written above grade level, which is usually determined by vocabulary and sentence length. Even when the texts are at grade level, not all the students are. Most troublesome is that the writing style is often disjointed. Few sentences or phrases clarify how one idea is connected to another, and stray facts, unrelated to the main idea, are seemingly stuck into paragraphs. This is called lack of textual coherence, which includes both global and local coherence (Richardson and Morgan 2000).

Middle- and upper-grade teachers often mistakenly assume that because reading is taught in the language arts classes, students are able to read expository texts without further instruction.

Texts with global coherence have clear major ideas so readers can follow the main concepts without becoming confused or sidetracked. Texts are organized by a logical pattern and do not mix narrative with expositional styles without cueing the reader. Texts with local coherence include relationship cues within sentences and paragraphs or between sentences and paragraphs. Without clear cues to how ideas are connected, students are left to fill in the relationships by themselves. The problem is that the content is new, and readers do not have enough background information to fill in those gaps. The text does not supply enough prompts about the relationships to allow the information to be grouped. Students are often left trying to learn the information in a laundry list fashion by rote memory.

Middle- and upper-grade teachers often mistakenly assume that because reading is taught in the language arts classes, students are able to read expository texts without further instruction. Although students come prepared with many strategies, they may not be the strategies required for textbook reading. Students have considerably less exposure to expository writing than to narrative writing at the primary levels; they are unfamiliar with the format.

Using Guided Reading with Content Texts

Using guided reading with content textbooks can be extremely valuable for teaching content and for teaching strategies for reading expository text. The procedure is much the same (see Figure 7.1). The teacher selects a short pasage for students to read. The teacher then asks a question of major importance, helping students identify the main concept and perhaps alerting them that the section they are about to read contains the concept and several examples. Students can be given a partially completed outline or graphic organizer that previews the organization of the chapter. The graphic organizer can be geared for textbooks, which are most commonly presented in a topic/subtopic format, so the students become familiar with the expository format. See Figure 7.2 for a sample of a basic graphic organizer for textbooks, also provided as a blackline master at the end of this chapter. Graphic organizers can also be related to a specific lesson. Using graphic organizers provides the students with a conceptual framework so they understand the relationships among the ideas. Graphic organizers are discussed again later in this chapter.

The teacher then leads a brief discussion of the content so new concepts are discussed in context, background knowledge is activated, and the subject is placed within a wider scope. Students best learn and remember new information when it is integrated with relevant prior knowledge or existing schemata (Pearson et al. 1999). Some students seem to think school subjects are to be mastered during the school day and have no relationship to the rest of their lives. Letting students know where in the real world this knowledge is useful or how it relates to the students' personal lives provides motivation.

The Guided Reading Process for Textbooks and Expository Texts

SELECT

The teacher selects a short passage for students to read.

BACKGROUND

The teacher briefly explains the content; new concepts are discussed in context, background knowledge is activated, and the subject is placed within a wider scope.

PURPOSE

The teacher asks a question to help students identify the main concept and alert students that the section they are about to read contains the concept and several examples.

READ

The students read the passage silently.

DISCUSSION

The teacher and the students discuss the concept right away and clarify misunderstandings.

QUESTION

The teacher can use special qualities of the text or strategies students need to learn to determine the types of questions to ask. The teacher also asks students how they determined the relationships between the ideas.

Figure 7.1

After the teacher sets the purpose and activitates background knowledge, the students read the section silently, looking for the concept and distinguishing the primary explanation from the examples. After everyone has finished reading, the teacher and the students discuss the concept right away and clarify misunderstandings. As students read and discuss sections, the teacher can ask them how they determined the relationships between the ideas. As students give their answers, they develop the strategy of using the organizational clues in a textbook such as charts and headings. Teachers can use

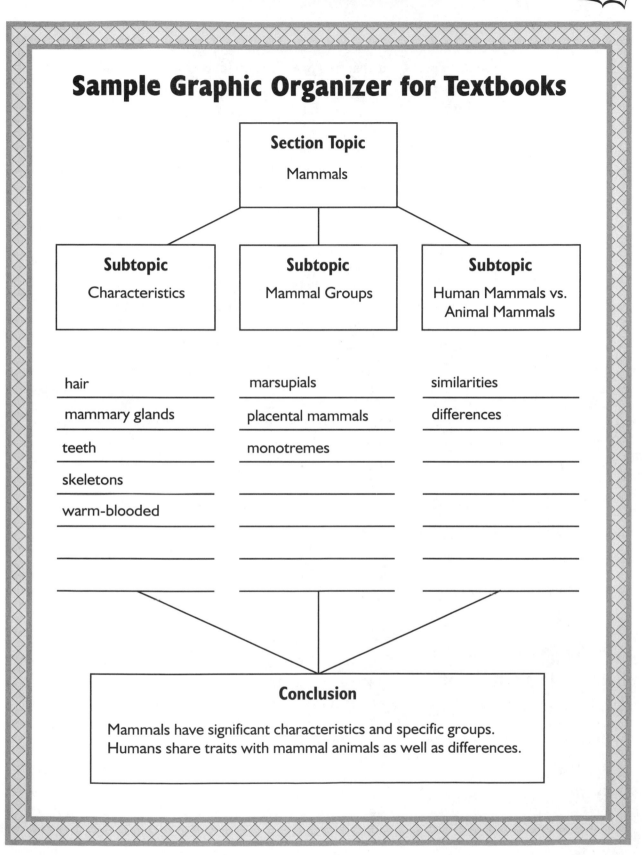

Sample Graphic Organizer for Textbooks

Section Topic

Mammals

Subtopic

Characteristics

Subtopic

Mammal Groups

Subtopic

Human Mammals vs. Animal Mammals

hair

mammary glands

teeth

skeletons

warm-blooded

marsupials

placental mammals

monotremes

similarities

differences

Conclusion

Mammals have significant characteristics and specific groups. Humans share traits with mammal animals as well as differences.

Figure 7.2

special qualities of the text or strategies students need to learn to determine the types of questions to ask. Students can also be asked to retrieve information from the graphs and charts so readers learn to use the graphic aids effectively. This certainly beats the round-robin oral reading of texts still found in many classrooms.

Here is an example of the traditional process gone astray when students were asked to read silently and then answer questions. The selection, similar to the following, was about predicting earthquakes.

> What causes earthquakes? When there is an earthquake the surface of the earth, called the crust, is pushed or stretched until it breaks. The surface of the earth, scientists believe, is made up of large plates which are moving constantly but very slowly. When they move, they stretch or squeeze the rocks of the earth's surface at the edges of the plates until the rocks finally shift and break apart, causing an earthquake. The line where the earth's crust breaks is called a fault.

After the students finished reading, the teacher asked them to write the answers to several questions, including "What causes earthquakes?" She even tried to give a strategy hint: "The answers are right there in the text. Find them. These are not inferences." A student answered, "I think it is where there is a pulse or wave of electricity that kind of explodes and opens a crack." If the class had used guided reading for this section, the teacher could have asked the student to cite the lines that proved her answer. Finding this difficult, the student could have been guided to the correct heading and located the appropriate lines. The student would have left with the correct impression about the content and a strategy for how to uncover an answer. As it was, the student's misconception continued until the papers were corrected. By then the class had moved on to the next topic. Students' schemata are very strong, even those that are incorrect. If they have misconceptions, such as thinking waves of electricity cause earthquakes, they are hesitant to give up their notions even when facing contradictory information in the text (Pearson et al. 1999). Post-reading or guided reading discussions that ask students to compare what they had thought about a topic to what they found in the text can help overcome these misconceptions.

Some students seem to think school subjects are to be mastered during the school day and have no relationship to the rest of their lives. Letting students know where in the real world this knowledge is useful or how it relates to the students' personal lives provides motivation.

Variations for Reading Content Texts

In addition to conventional guided reading techniques, other variations that can be used with expository text are discussed in the following sections. Some have been developed just for use with expository text. The variations include ReQuest, Questioning the Author (QtA), Talking Drawings, critical reading, and study guides. Special issues about critical reading in the content areas and a reintroduction to the study guide—an old favorite with some new goals—as a virtual guided reading teacher in the content areas follow.

ReQuest

One strategy that can be used with content texts is ReQuest (Manzo as cited in Richardson and Morgan 2000). The teacher and students silently read a short section. The students ask the teacher questions about the text. The students are instructed to ask the types of questions that a teacher might ask (Stier 2000). The teacher must answer the students' questions without using the book. The teacher can model strategies that integrate knowledge or show how an answer was developed. When the students' questions are exhausted, the teacher asks questions, and the students answer with their books closed. Teacher and students answer all questions as fully and honestly as possible; both can refer back to the text to prove their answers or clarify a point. At first, the teacher's questions will probably be at higher levels of comprehension than the students' questions.

The ReQuest session will follow a pattern when applied to expository texts. The first section in an expository text will probably be an introduction. If the text is well written, this section will include previews of examples or subtopics that will be developed later in the text. The introduction is perfect for the question: "What do you think will be in the next section?" This type of question helps students anticipate the structure of a textbook. After the first round of questions are answered, the class reads another section and question each other again. The second set of ReQuest questions should set the purpose for reading the rest of the section. If not, the teacher can directly state a purpose for continued reading or ask the students what they think will occur in the next section. When the teacher thinks the students have a solid foundation for reading the rest of the text, the back-and-forth questioning ends, and the students read independently (see Figure 7.3).

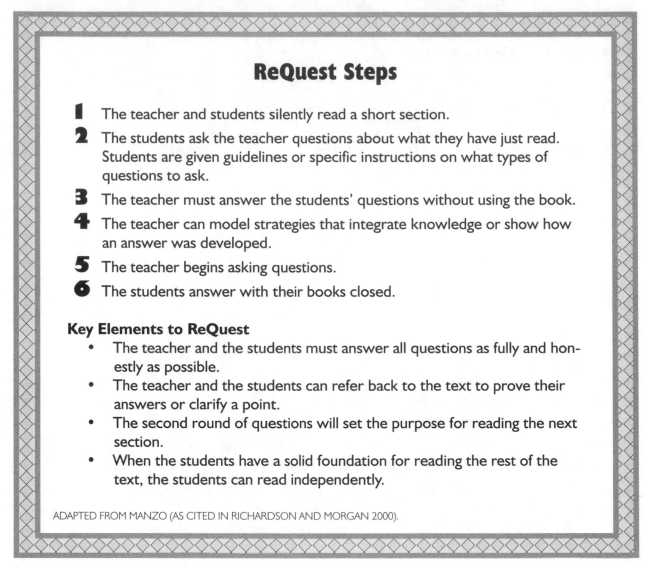

ReQuest Steps

1 The teacher and students silently read a short section.

2 The students ask the teacher questions about what they have just read. Students are given guidelines or specific instructions on what types of questions to ask.

3 The teacher must answer the students' questions without using the book.

4 The teacher can model strategies that integrate knowledge or show how an answer was developed.

5 The teacher begins asking questions.

6 The students answer with their books closed.

Key Elements to ReQuest

- The teacher and the students must answer all questions as fully and honestly as possible.
- The teacher and the students can refer back to the text to prove their answers or clarify a point.
- The second round of questions will set the purpose for reading the next section.
- When the students have a solid foundation for reading the rest of the text, the students can read independently.

ADAPTED FROM MANZO (AS CITED IN RICHARDSON AND MORGAN 2000).

Figure 7.3

Students can improve in question formation and comprehension rather quickly. A study (May 1998) describes a group of fourth- and fifth-graders who participated in nine days of training. The teacher modeled questions related to a reading passage on the first day. Students then practiced in a whole-class setting for three days and in five- to six-member cooperative groups for three days. For the last two days, students worked in pairs or alone. The students significantly outperformed a control group on comprehension because they self-questioned as they read. The more often ReQuest is used and the more often teachers articulate the types of questions they are asking and the strategies for finding answers, the more proficient students will become in asking sophisticated questions that will eventually be used for self-questioning.

Questioning the Author (QtA)

Questioning the Author (QtA), developed by Isabel Beck, Margaret McKeown, Rebecca Hamilton, and Linda Kucan (1999), is "designed to get students to build understanding of text ideas by becoming actively involved as they read, by diving into difficult information and grappling to make sense of it" (372). In earlier studies, Beck and her colleagues found that texts were often poorly written and authors of the texts presumed that students had greater background knowledge than they actually did. The researchers experimented with rewriting texts to make the connections more explicit. As they revised the books, they uncovered methods that they themselves used to supplement the disjointed text. QtA teaches students those same constructivist techniques of combining text information with what the reader already knows in terms of language, text structures, and information to make the text more understandable. The name QtA describes the strategy of students questioning the author's intended meaning because sometimes ideas are not written as clearly as authors thought they were.

Teachers must plan the lesson by reading the text themselves, identifying main concepts to be learned, and anticipating what problems an inexperienced reader might have, especially in terms of general background knowledge needed to understand the text. Teachers divide the chapter into smaller sections, stopping at major points or where difficulties are likely to occur. With the smaller sections, students can conquer the text one major idea at a time. As with guided reading, first-time reading is tackled in class, which allows students to hear one another's opinions, test their own viewpoints, learn how others use strategies to unravel the text, and receive guidance from the teacher as they read. See Figure 7.4 for an outline of QtA.

The main strategy of QtA is queries. Queries are questions that are designed to assist students in grappling with text ideas. They are unlike questions in a traditional classroom discussion, which are aimed at assessing student comprehension. Instead of just a student-teacher interchange, queries are meant to facilitate group discussion. Queries

> **With guided reading, first-time reading is tackled in class, which allows students to hear one another's opinions, test their own viewpoints, learn how others use strategies to unravel the text, and receive guidance from the teacher as they read.**

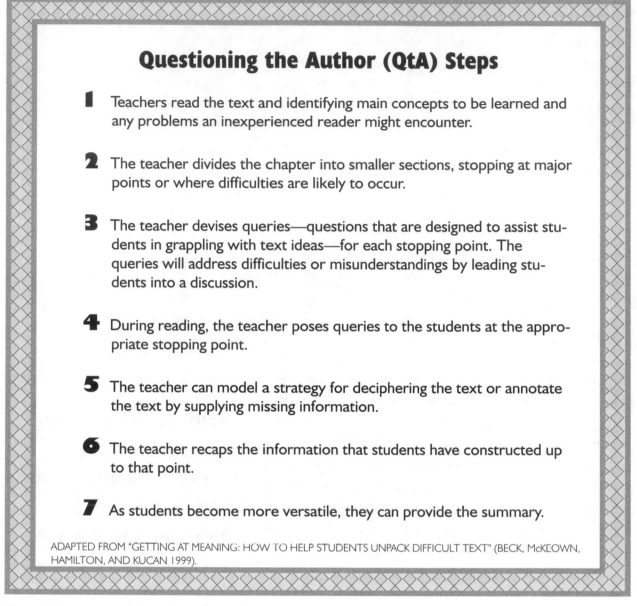

Questioning the Author (QtA) Steps

1 Teachers read the text and identifying main concepts to be learned and any problems an inexperienced reader might encounter.

2 The teacher divides the chapter into smaller sections, stopping at major points or where difficulties are likely to occur.

3 The teacher devises queries—questions that are designed to assist students in grappling with text ideas—for each stopping point. The queries will address difficulties or misunderstandings by leading students into a discussion.

4 During reading, the teacher poses queries to the students at the appropriate stopping point.

5 The teacher can model a strategy for deciphering the text or annotate the text by supplying missing information.

6 The teacher recaps the information that students have constructed up to that point.

7 As students become more versatile, they can provide the summary.

ADAPTED FROM "GETTING AT MEANING: HOW TO HELP STUDENTS UNPACK DIFFICULT TEXT" (BECK, McKEOWN, HAMILTON, AND KUCAN 1999).

Figure 7.4

encourage students to build from one another's answers and offer varying aspects of a topic in their own words. While traditional instruction takes place after reading, queries are used during reading. Queries act to supplement the text and connect muddled facts and concepts.

It is difficult to explain the difference between a question and a query. A query, in this case, really probes the author's text and digs into the implied meaning. The focus changes from finding a right answer—that is, repeating correctly what the author said—to connecting the answer to other concepts.

Beck and her colleagues provide examples from a social studies book that help explain the difference. A question is "What did the early Hawaiians eat?", which is answered with "Sweet potatoes and breadfruit." On the other hand, a query is "What does the author mean by 'they began to raise plants'?" The query is derived from the first line of the text, "When the Polynesians settled on the Hawaiian Islands, they began to raise plants that they had brought with them." The answers turned into a discussion of growing food and why supplies brought with the Polynesians would not last and how they could be renewable.

General queries are "What is the author trying to say here?" or "What is the author's message?" Follow-up queries can be "Does the author explain this clearly? Does this make sense with what the author told us before?" or "Does the author tell us why?" For particularly difficult passages, the teacher can model a strategy for deciphering the text or annotate the text by supplying missing information. Finally, the teacher recaps the information that students have constructed up to that point. As students become more versatile, they can provide the summary.

As adults, it is sometimes difficult to compose queries. The lines in the text seem so obvious because we possess far greater background knowledge and can almost unconsciously fill in the missing connections. Students, however, often read at a shallow, unconnected level, and nothing is obvious beyond the words on the page, which they will happily repeat and promptly forget. The querying process can be very slow, but reading with deep comprehension and making connections to other concepts and information is too often sacrificed for covering the curriculum. Even then, the curriculum is often covered to about the depth of a grain of sand and blown away just about as easily.

What are Queries?

◆ Queries are questions that are designed to assist students in grappling with text ideas.

◆ Queries are meant to facilitate group discussion.

◆ Queries encourage students to build on one another's answers.

◆ Queries offer varying aspects of a topic in students' own words.

◆ Queries are used during reading.

◆ Queries supplement the text and connect facts and concepts.

◆ Queries explore the author's implied meaning.

◆ Queries focus on connecting the answer to other concepts.

General Queries

◆ What is the author trying to say here?

◆ What is the author's message?

Follow-up Queries

◆ Does the author explain this clearly?

◆ Does this make sense with what the author told us before?

◆ Does the author tell us why?

Talking Drawings

Talking Drawings (Wood 2001) seems deceptively simple. First, teachers ask students to draw the topic or event to be studied. They can make a simple or complex sketch. Students then share their drawings and talk about and analyze why they depicted the topic as they did. A student can write a concept map on the board as collective prior knowledge accumulates. Conflicts might appear. The students then read the passage and redraw the event or topic. The class discusses changes from previous conceptions and beliefs. Students must then individually write what they changed about their before and after pictures. This is a particularly good intervention for clearing up misconceptions. Although this procedure does not provide during-reading guidance, it is a good technique for students who are gradually being released from direct teacher supervision. There is still activation of prior knowledge before reading and an immediate check after reading. Best of all, students must probe their own prior knowledge and make adjustments after reading. See Figure 7.5 for Talking Drawings steps.

Study Guides

Study guides can act as a virtual guided reading teacher. Study guides fit many formats, but are usually a group of questions that a teacher prepares to help direct students' attention to the major points in the textbook. They can be just plain questions, fill-in-the-blank questions, a blank graphic organizer, or a make-your-own graphic organizer. Most study guides help students find the most important parts of the text while monitoring that the students actually read the text. They can list hints and strategy reminders in addition to questions.

The study guide can help students see organizational text patterns and how one piece of information fits with another.

On a fundamental level, the study guide can help students see organizational text patterns and how one piece of information fits with another. This is particularly important for students who have only a narrative schema. Study guides can help students determine the importance of ideas and differentiate between main ideas and details and examples. They can help students use the special features of text such as headings and subheadings and the various graphic aids that students usually ignore.

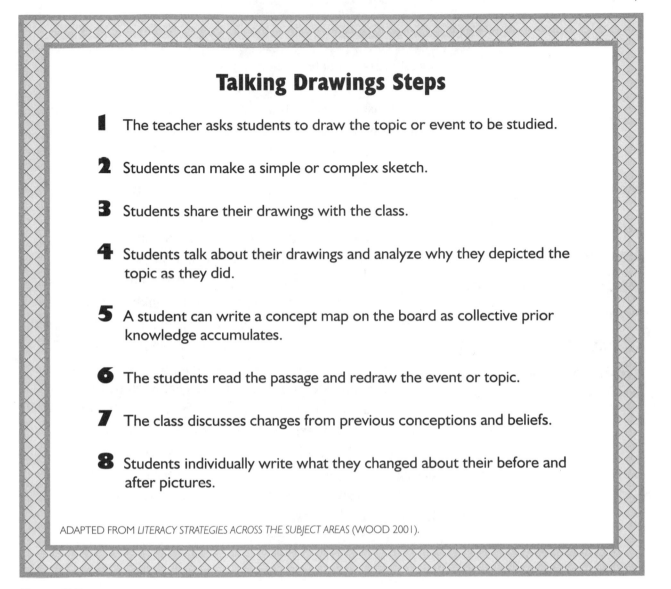

Talking Drawings Steps

1 The teacher asks students to draw the topic or event to be studied.

2 Students can make a simple or complex sketch.

3 Students share their drawings with the class.

4 Students talk about their drawings and analyze why they depicted the topic as they did.

5 A student can write a concept map on the board as collective prior knowledge accumulates.

6 The students read the passage and redraw the event or topic.

7 The class discusses changes from previous conceptions and beliefs.

8 Students individually write what they changed about their before and after pictures.

ADAPTED FROM *LITERACY STRATEGIES ACROSS THE SUBJECT AREAS* (WOOD 2001).

Figure 7.5

On an advanced level, teachers can ask students to make connections between the text, concepts, and their lives. For these questions, it is best to ask a few well-chosen questions that will be fully answered rather than many questions. See Figure 7.6 for a sample graphic organizer for cause and effect. The teacher has supplied causes and effects and students are asked to fill in the corresponding causes and effects. See Figure 7.7 for a sample study guide graphic organizer for comparison and contrast. In this organizer, the teacher has supplied the two main topics and the headings and the students have filled in the rest. To get started, the teacher might also fill in some examples or lead a class discussion to begin filling in the organizer. (Blackline masters for Figures 7.6 and 7.7 are also provided at the end of this chapter.)

Critical Reading in Content Texts

Many students still seem to believe their job is only to memorize the facts and definitions and repeat them for the teacher. We expect young people to learn the lessons of history or the ethics of science and apply them to a lifetime of sound decision making and citizenship with integrity. Teaching students to question at the critical level gives them an opportunity to begin considering issues that affect their lives and their society. This examination of content and its implications, through self-questioning, questioning of the author, or classroom discussion, does not occur serendipitously; it occurs through planning and instruction by the teacher. Teachers should remember that "It is not fair to expect that students can become autonomous in thinking and learning without the benefit of instruction" (Richardson and Morgan 2000). Teachers should gradually release responsibility to their students so they can become independent learners. This independence is the ultimate goal of guided reading.

Guided reading provides structure and clues about the purpose, organization, and style of expository text. It invites students to integrate their previous knowledge with new text information. It provides models of constructing meaning so students can learn to read and comprehend independently. Guided reading can and should be used to develop critical thinking skills in the content areas.

> **Teaching students to question at the critical level gives them an opportunity to begin considering issues that affect their lives and their society.**

Sample Cause and Effect Graphic Organizer for Content Reading

Cause	Effect
1. President Jefferson hoped to claim a water route to the Pacific Northwest so . . .	1.
2.	2. . . . so Lewis began ordering knives, tomahawks, rifles, gunpowder, and an iron framework boat.
3.	3. . . . so Lewis began a crash course in navigation and astronomy.
4. The river was low and the boat heavily laden when they reached the shoal so . . .	4.
5.	5. . . . so Jefferson knew Lewis and Clark's position in the winter of 1803–1804.
6.	6. . . . so the departure was delayed until May 14.
7. All of the tribes of the lower Missouri had been out hunting buffalo in late July and early August so . . .	7.
8.	8. . . . so each member of the party consumed up to nine pounds of meat per day, whatever fruit could be found, and some cornmeal.
9. Shannon, separated from the party for 16 days, thought the boats were ahead of him so . . .	9.

Figure 7.6

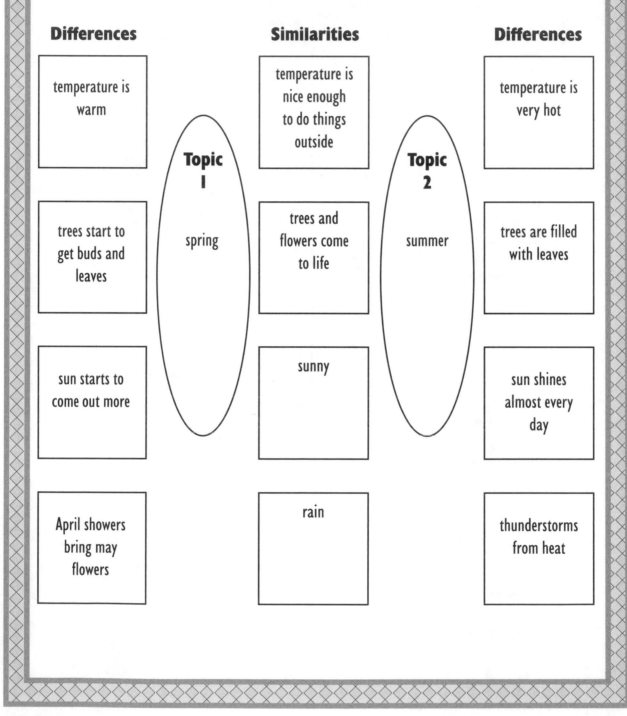

Sample Graphic Organizer
for Comparison and Contrast

Differences		Similarities		Differences
temperature is warm		temperature is nice enough to do things outside		temperature is very hot
trees start to get buds and leaves	**Topic 1** spring	trees and flowers come to life	**Topic 2** summer	trees are filled with leaves
sun starts to come out more		sunny		sun shines almost every day
April showers bring may flowers		rain		thunderstorms from heat

Figure 7.7

Chapter Seven Summary

The drawback to guided reading in the content areas is that it is very time-consuming. However, the choice may be between mastering some content in depth while learning to use a text independently for future self-instruction or learning a lot of content superficially without having any strategies for self-instruction.

TEACHER QUOTE

❝ Guided reading is an excellent strategy for teaching reading comprehension. It enables me to monitor student comprehension during reading. Guided reading is especially effective when the students are reading novels. It can also be easily adapted for expository text. Guided reading is easy to implement and no extra planning time is required. ❞

—Marilyn Winton
5th grade teacher
Greenwood School
Woodstock, IL

Chapter 7 Blackline Masters

◆ Graphic Organizers for Content Reading
- Graphic Organizer for Textbooks
- Cause and Effect Graphic Organizer
- Comparison and Contrast Graphic Organizer

◆ Ideas for Classroom Use
- Make an overhead transparency and photocopies for each student of the graphic organizer for textbooks. Select a short passage for students to read. (Be sure the passage is introductory and includes the main topic.) Lead students to the main topic by asking them probing question. Students can fill in the conclusion on their own, with partners, in small groups, or after a whole-class discussion.
- Fill out a cause and effect for each line on the Cause and Effect Graphic Organizer. Give a copy to each student or pair. Read the text as a class until you reach the first cause and effect. Model for students how to discover the cause and effect and how to use the organizer. Ask students to read the text and complete the causes and effects.
- Choose a passage that compares and contrasts two topics. Give each student a copy of the Comparison and Contrast Graphic Organizer. Provide two topics to compare and contrast and have students write these topics on the organizer. Read a portion of text as a class. Ask students to locate differences and similarities between the two topics. (Explain that similarities and/or differences may not be clearly stated.) Model how to use the organizer. Ask students to read the rest of the text and fill in the organizer.

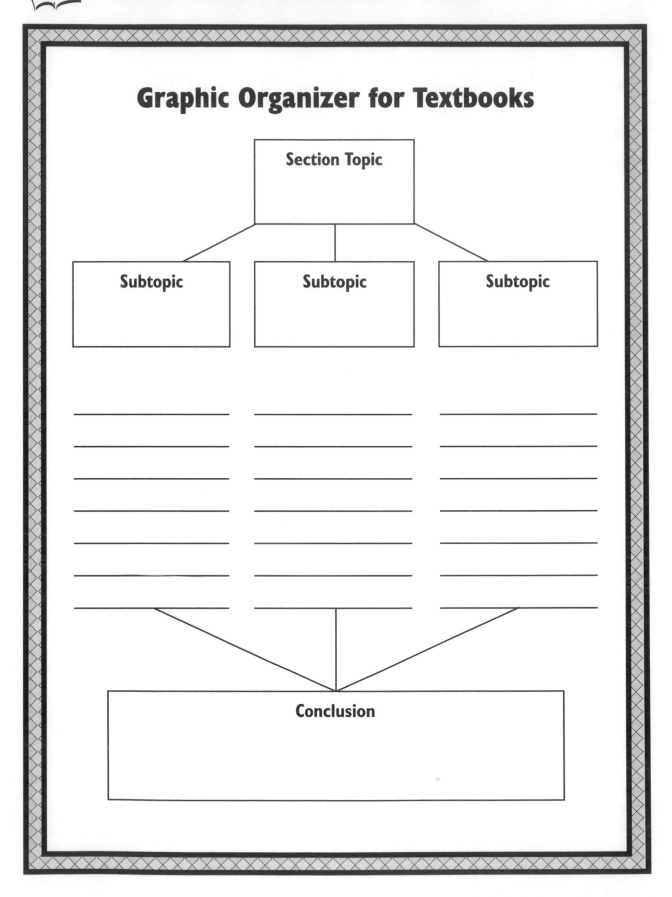

Graphic Organizer for Textbooks

Section Topic

Subtopic   **Subtopic**   **Subtopic**

Conclusion

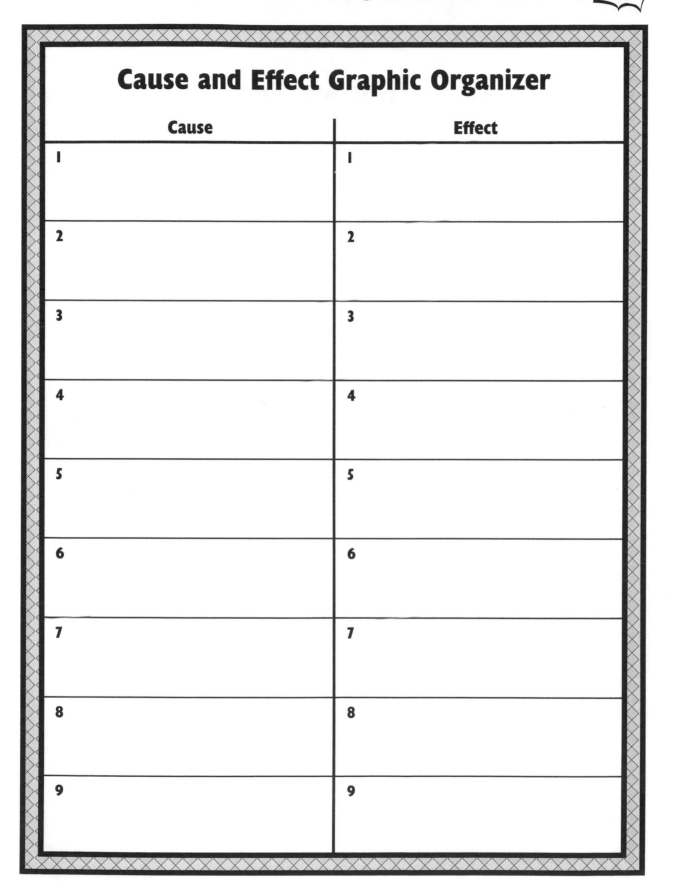

Cause and Effect Graphic Organizer

Cause	Effect
1	1
2	2
3	3
4	4
5	5
6	6
7	7
8	8
9	9

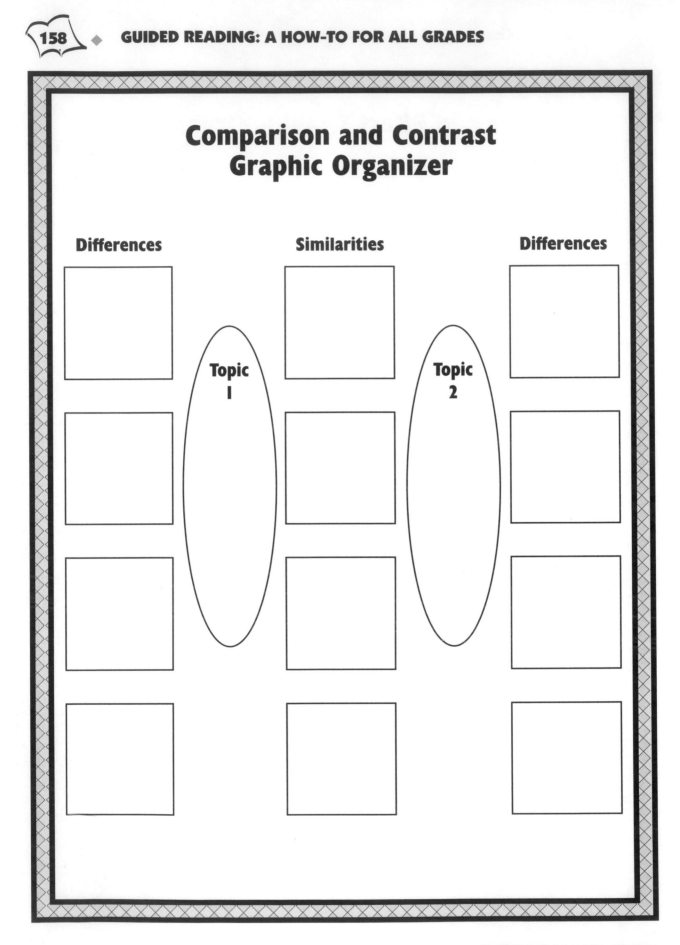

Comparison and Contrast Graphic Organizer

Differences   **Similarities**   **Differences**

Topic 1

Topic 2

Final Thoughts

uided reading is one of the most important techniques a teacher can use throughout all the grades. In the primary grades, guided reading takes the form of interactive read-alouds and small guided reading groups with leveled books. Small guided reading groups provide the opportunity for the teacher to be in the right place at the right time with materials at the right level. There are few times during the day when students can receive such personalized instruction. The continuous diagnosis through observation and running records make it possible for students to remain at the right level with just a little challenge so they can use problem-solving skills.

In the grades 3–12, guided reading helps students identify and apply comprehension strategies to the stories and textbooks that they are actually using. Although guided reading is very time-consuming, most of the unrelated (and usually dull) practice materials can be eliminated, and students see the immediate relevancy of learning comprehension strategies. Another benefit is that everyone in the class can be included in the same novel or the same textbook chapter because the teacher provides continuous scaffolding or guidance throughout guided reading. This is critically important for students who are unfamiliar with using expository text for learning new information and concepts.

The goal of guided reading—supporting readers on their way to becoming independent—is always the same, although there are several variations to the process. Variations include ReQuest, Questioning the Author, reciprocal reading, or the venerable Directed Reading Thinking Activity. The variations are what add spice to reading instruction and show students how to tackle the problems of comprehension from several angles.

Best of all, students who struggle the most benefit the most from guided reading. The best readers almost learn by themselves, are self-motivated by their success, and need less support and guidance. Through guided reading, struggling readers find a means to be successful. With books that are a little hard, but not impossible, the teacher points out reading strategies that the students are using or could be using to understand the story or learn new content. Content and process are interwoven. By practicing with the help of a teacher, struggling readers learn what expert readers do and become more confident and capable. Soon they are on the road to becoming independent readers who actually like to read and know what they are doing. Teachers benefit from guided reading as well, feeling successful and competent as they share their expertise and guide students to discover the joy of reading.

Bibliography

Almansi, J. 1995. The nature of fourth graders' sociocognitive conflicts in peer-led and teacher-led discussions of literature. *Reading Research Quarterly.* 30: 314–51.

Barrentine, S. J. 1996. Engaging with reading through interactive read-alouds. *The Reading Teacher.* 50(1): 26–43.

Beck, I. L., M. G. McKeown, R. L. Hamilton, and L. Kucan. 1999. Getting at the meaning: How to help students unpack difficult text. In *Read all about it: Reading to inform the profession,* 371–80. Sacramento, CA: California State Board of Education.

———.1998, Spring/Summer. Getting at the meaning. *American Educator,* 66–85.

Borgert, S. 1998. *Learning to read . . . reading to learn.* http://www.cs. oswego.edu/~borgert/Html/Newsletters/january-1998.html (Accessed Nov. 29, 2000.)

Bruce, C., D. Snodgrass, and J. Salzman. 1999. *A tale of two methods: Melding project read and guided reading to improve at-risk students' literacy skills.* Paper presented at the Mid-Western Educational Research Association, October, 1999, Chicago, IL.

Davey, B. 1983. Think aloud: Modeling the cognitive processes of reading comprehension. *Journal of Reading.* 27(1): 44–47.

Fawson, P. C., and D. R. Reutzel. 2000. But I only have a basal: Implementing guided reading in the early grades. *The Reading Teacher.* 54(1):84–97.

Fountas, I. C., and G. S. Pinnell. 1996. *Guided reading: Good first teaching for all children.* Portsmouth, NH: Heinemann.

Goodman, Y., and C. L. Burke. 1972. *Reading miscue inventory manual: Procedure for diagnosis and evaluation.* New York: Macmillan.

Graves, M. F., and B. B. Graves. 1994. *Scaffolding reading experiences: Designs for student success.* Norwood, MA: Christopher-Gordon.

Graves, M. F., C. Juel, and B. B. Graves. 1998. *Teaching reading in the 21st century*. Boston: Allyn & Bacon.

Gunning, T. G. 2000. *Best books for building literacy for elementary school children.* Boston: Allyn & Bacon.

Joyce, B., and B. Showers. 1995. *Student achievement through staff development.* White Plaines, NY: Longman.

Kucan, L., and I. Beck. 1997. Thinking aloud and reading comprehension research: Inquiry, instruction, and social interaction. *Review of Educational Research* 67: 271–99.

Langenberg, D. N., chair. 2000. *Report of the national reading panel.* Rockville, MD: National Institute of Child Health and Human Development.

May, F. 1998. *Reading as communication: To help children write and read.* Upper Saddle River, NJ: Merrill.

Mooney, M. 1995a. Guided reading beyond the primary grades. *Teaching K–8.* (1): 75–77.

———. 1995b. Guided reading—The reader in control. *Teaching K–8.* 25(5): 54–58.

———.1990. *Reading to, with, and by children*. Katonah, NY: Richard C. Owen.

Nessel, D. 1989. Do your students think when they read? *Learning.* 17(8): 54–58.

Palincsar, A. S., and A. L. Brown. 1984. Teaching of comprehension and monitoring activities. *Cognition and Instruction.* 1(2): 117–75.

Pearson, P. D., L. R. Roehler, J. Dole, and G. Duffy. 1999. Developing expertise in reading comprehension. In *Read all about it: Reading to inform the profession,* 381–409. Sacramento: California State Board of Education.

Perkins, D., and G. Salomon. 1992. The science and art of transfer. In *If minds matter I,* edited by A. Costa, J. Bellanca, and R. Fogarty, 201–10. Palatine, IL: IRI/Skylight Training and Publishing.

Potter, B. 1955. The tale of Peter Rabbit. In *The illustrated treasury of children's literature,* edited by M. E. Martignoni, 46–48. New York: Grosset & Dunlap.

Raphael, T. E. 1986. Teaching question-answer relationships revisited. *The Reading Teacher.* 39: 516–22.

Raphael, T. E., and P. D. Pearson. 1982 . *The effect of metacognitive awareness training on children's question-answering behavior*. Tech. Rep. No. 238. Urbana, IL: University of Illinois, Center for the Study of Reading.

Richardson, J. S., and R. F. Morgan. 2000. *Reading to learn in the content areas.* 4th edition. Belmont, CA: Wadsworth Thomson Learning.

Richek, M. A. 1987. DRTA: 5 variations that facilitate independence in reading narratives. *Journal of Reading.* 30: 632–36.

Roberts, K. L. 1940. *Hoyt's new cyclopedia of practical quotations.* New York: Grosset & Dunlap.

Routman, R. 1991. *Invitations: Changing as teachers and learners K–12.* Portsmouth, NH: Heinemann.

Rowling, J. K. 1997. *Harry Potter and the sorcerer's stone.* New York: Scholastic.

Schulman, M. B., and C. D. Payne. 2000. *Guided reading: Making it work.* New York: Scholastic.

Snow, C. E., M. S. Burns, and P. Griffin, eds. 1998. *Preventing reading difficulties in young children.* National Research Council. Washington, D.C.: National Academy Press.

Speare, E. G. 1983. *The sign of the beaver.* New York: Yearling.

Stanovich, K. 1993–94. Romance and reality. *The Reading Teacher.* 47: 208–91.

Stauffer, R. 1969. *Teaching reading as a thinking process.* New York: Harper & Row.

Stevenson, R. L. 1939. *Treasure island.* New York: Charles Scribner's Sons.

Stier, F. 2000. Request reciprocal teaching. *AskERIC Lesson Plans.* http:// ericir.syr.edu/Virtual/Lessons/Lang_arts/Reading/RDG0006.html (Accessed Nov. 29, 2000.)

Taylor, M. 1977. *Roll of thunder, hear my cry.* New York: Dial.

Taylor, T. 1969. *The cay.* New York: Avon Camelot.

Tierney, R. J., and J. E. Readence. 2000. *Reading strategies and practices: A compendium.* 5th edition. Boston: Allyn & Bacon.

Tompkins, G. E. 1997. *Literacy for the twenty-first century: A balanced approach.* Upper Saddle River, NJ: Merrill.

White, E. B. 1952. *Charlotte's web.* New York: Harper & Row.

Wood, K. 2001. *Literacy strategies across the subject areas.* Boston: Allyn & Bacon.

Index